# A Settler's Year

# A SETTLER'S YEAR

## PIONEER LIFE THROUGH THE SEASONS

**KATHLEEN ERNST**

Photographs by LOYD HEATH

WISCONSIN HISTORICAL SOCIETY PRESS

Published by the Wisconsin Historical Society Press
*Publishers since 1855*

Text copyright © Kathleen Ernst, LLC, 2015

For permission to reuse material from *A Settler's Year: Pioneer Life through the Seasons* (ISBN 978-0-87020-714-3 and e-book ISBN 978-0-87020-715-0), please access www.copyright.com or contact the Copyright Clearance Center, Inc. (CCC), 222 Rosewood Drive, Danvers, MA 01923, 978-750-8400. CCC is a not-for-profit organization that provides licenses and registration for a variety of users.

**wisconsinhistory.org**

Photographs identified with WHi or WHS are from the Society's collections; address requests to reproduce these photos to the Visual Materials Archivist at the Wisconsin Historical Society, 816 State Street, Madison, WI 53706.

Photographs copyright © Loyd Heath 2015 unless otherwise credited
Printed in the United States of America
Designed by Percolator Graphic Design

19  18  17  16  15     1  2  3  4  5

Library of Congress Cataloging-in-Publication Data

Ernst, Kathleen, 1959–
    A settler's year : pioneer life through the seasons / Kathleen Ernst ; photographs by Loyd Heath.
        pages cm
    Includes bibliographical references and index.
    ISBN 978-0-87020-714-3 (hardcover : alk. paper)—ISBN 978-0-87020-715-0 (ebook)
1. Frontier and pioneer life—Wisconsin. 2. Wisconsin—History—19th century.
    I. Heath, Loyd. II. Title.
    F584.E76 2015
    977.5′03—dc23
                2015005242

♾ The paper used in this publication meets the minimum requirements of the American National Standard for Information Sciences—Permanence of Paper for Printed Library Materials, ANSI Z39.48-1992.

*In memory of Marty Perkins:*
*scholar, colleague, mentor, friend*

# CONTENTS

# INTRODUCTION

On a breezy, salt-scented day in the nineteenth century, a group of Bohemian immigrants with tearstained cheeks leaned over the railing of the ship that would take them to America. Someone began to sing "Where Is My Home?" Husky-voiced, the others joined in as their last glimpse of Europe faded into the horizon behind them.

Another day, an Irish boy with haunted eyes and hollow cheeks boarded a ship. He did not look back at the land so desperately ravaged by potato blight and famine. Pinned inside his pocket was the note his mother had scribbled on a scrap of paper before she died—the name of an unknown uncle, and a single compass word: *Wisconsin*.

At a different dock, several German women gave the tail ends of fat balls of homespun wool to their weeping, shawl-wrapped mothers and sisters. The yarn unwound behind the immigrants as they trudged up the gangway to their ship and found space at the railing. When the ship left her moorings, the yarn unspooled all too fast through trembling fingers. Soon each woman on the deck felt her twisted filament slip away—the last ephemeral link to everything dear and familiar. Dozens of strands billowed lightly over the water, fading from sight like the tail of some fearful mare galloping back to familiar pastures.

Sometime later a deeply indebted Swedish tenant farmer slipped ghostlike from home on a dark night and made his way to the nearest port. He left his family with nothing but a promise to send passage money when he could. Years would pass before the family could reunite.

Where is my home?

The question haunted thousands of Europeans a century and more ago. They were caught between all they had ever known and the unimaginable—a new life on a different continent. Might America's dazzling possibilities truly justify leaving loved ones forever? The decision was agonizing. Johann Schuster of Bavaria succumbed to gnawing doubts before departure: "We know how things are here," he cried. "Germany we know; America is an unknown country to us." His wife replied, kindly but firmly, "Johann, we leave tomorrow for America."[1]

*Some women spent months deciding how to squeeze necessities and mementos into sturdy wooden trunks. Others arrived in the New World with baskets and unwieldy bundles. All of them packed— in addition to wool socks, linen sheets, dried peas—dreams of a better life.* (WHI IMAGE ID 4722)

*Women struggled to keep their infants and toddlers clean, healthy, and safe during the long trip. Sea voyages meant cramped quarters, seasickness, and fresh water doled out in strictly rationed portions. Many mothers were homesick, worried, and exhausted before even beginning the journey from the Atlantic coast to Wisconsin.* (WHI IMAGE ID 38123)

Some immigrants traveled alone; others took strength from friends, relatives, or neighbors who had chosen to journey together. They'd all gambled that the trip would lead to a better life—if not for them, for their children. In Wisconsin, the population rose from 11,000 to over 305,000 between 1836 and 1850. By then, one-third of the population was foreign-born—some from Great Britain, some from Europe.[2]

Behind the statistics were more than a hundred thousand unique people, each with her or his own hopes and heartaches. Schoolchildren can recite lists of "push and pull factors" that contributed to the mass immigration. Famine, wars and compulsory military service, political or religious oppression, lack of affordable or arable land, and primogeniture (which permitted only the eldest son to inherit land) prompted thousands of European children, women, and men to turn their backs on home and family; available land and glowing reports from early settlers and land agents lured them across the Atlantic. But many Polish immigrants, whose homeland was under Russian and German rule, summarized the reason for leaving succinctly: *za chlebem*—for bread. Thousands of desperate Poles saw no hope of preserving their culture, tilling their own land, or otherwise providing the most basic necessities for themselves and their children in the Old World. They came in search of a new home.

After surviving the ocean crossing, newcomers made the next leg of their journey in canal boats, sloops, or steamships; in rattling train cars or plodding wagons. Many aimed for Milwaukee, with its public lands office, opportunities for work, shops to replenish dwindling provisions, and growing pockets of ethnic settlement where many—especially Germans and Irish—took comfort in the cadence of familiar language.

And certainly, some of the immigrants stayed in Milwaukee or ultimately settled in other burgeoning cities. Tradesmen seeking new customers, men with money looking for commercial opportunities, men without money looking for work on the docks or in a brewery, tannery, or butcher shop—some settled into urban life for good. Most people, however, took a deep breath, squared their shoulders, and plunged into Wisconsin's prairies and woodlands. In 1850, less than 10 percent of Wisconsin's population were urban dwellers.[3]

Also traveling from the Eastern seaboard were Yankees—men and women of English descent, many third- or fourth-generation Americans. Perhaps restless, perhaps adventurous, perhaps already feeling confined by growing populations, perhaps frustrated by rising land prices, they left friends and family in Maine and Vermont and New York to try their luck on the western frontier.

Many of these families had packed the latest mechanical innovation into their wagons—a new harrow, or the latest hand-cranked sewing machine. They brought a zeal for civic improvements and a dedication to democratic government. Albert Tuttle, who left his wife and son in Connecticut while he explored Wisconsin, made clear in a letter home his desire to transport what he cherished most:

> Could we place here New England Institutions and hear echoing from these hill tops and swelling along these valleys the sound of the "church going bell," could we see scattered through the country . . . her village school houses and find here that cultivated and refined society which education moulded by principles of sound truth there produces, then should we have a paradise indeed. Much as I love . . . the hills and valleys of old Litchfield county, I would gladly bid them adieu and fix permanently my abode here.[4]

These dreamers were not the first here, of course. Early French explorers and traders had met the area's Native American groups without displacing them. The 1832 Black Hawk War provided a climax to the tragic clash between US government land policy and the Indians' way of life. With most Native people ultimately removed from *their* homes, white (and a few black) pioneers found land available. Tuttle recognized, at least to some degree, that his opportunity meant heartache for others. "I have felt indignant that civilization should spun [*sic*] them from her embrace, driving them without her borders, compelling them to brook the wrongs and insults of brutal and degraded white men," he wrote in 1847—a year before Wisconsin achieved statehood.[5]

In 1862, the Homestead Act brought more settlers to the Upper Midwest with the promise of 160 acres of public land in exchange for five years of continuous residency. In Wisconsin, 3,110,990 acres were claimed by 29,246 homesteaders.[6] And whether it was bartered from a land speculator in 1842, obtained from the government twenty years later, or purchased from a northern lumber company several decades after that, these newcomers wanted a place of their own.

European immigrants might arrive in July, when there was still time to look for shelter and land—and when hot weather, crowded conditions, and malnutrition contributed to devastating epidemics. But shivering families often didn't arrive until late fall, delayed by sulky Atlantic winds or other challenges. Even Yankees sometimes faced an inauspicious arrival, as noted by Isaac T. Smith:

> It was the 26th of November, 1835, that I first set foot in Wisconsin. The weather was extremely cold, with one foot of snow upon the ground; I was in company with some families, consisting of women and small children, some of the latter but a few months old. As we were compelled to camp out upon the ground, our first lesson of Wisconsin Pioneering was not the most agreeable. However, we made the best of it.[7]

Some of the newcomers were dazed, destitute, and completely dependent upon earlier arrivals. Families in ethnic enclaves especially experienced a constant shuffling and reshuffling to accommodate fellow countrymen and women who limped toward their cabins with empty bellies and pockets.

Settlers who did have precious cash in their wallets thrummed with the urgent need to find *their* land, *their* farm. They walked, drove, or rode over the countryside, eagerly exploring this new landscape. "I expected to see fine country," marveled Uriah S. Hollister in 1839, "but it is much more beautiful than I had any idea of."[8] Most also assessed what they saw with a practical eye. Europeans stared with awe at tracts of virgin timber and prairies unmarred by plow furrow, rail fence, or cabin. Incredulous farmers rubbed the rich soil between their fingers, sniffing the loam. "Without manure and with scarcely half the labor we would give to fields at home, it yields abundant crops of wheat, rye, barley, oats, melons, cabbage, kohlrabi, and other vegetables," wrote Søren Bache, a Norwegian who traveled through Illinois and on to Wisconsin in 1839.[9]

*German immigrant Christian Turck built this side-gabled home in Germantown in 1846. The house, which features a cantilevered porch hood, is an example of the German Blockbau building style. This photograph was taken several generations later, around 1900. In 1976 the house was moved to Old World Wisconsin. It is now known as the Schottler House. The Schottler family lived on the farm in 1875, the period interpreted at the historic site.* (WHI IMAGE ID 3988)

Swiss immigrant Mathias Duerst, who helped found New Glarus in 1845, was delighted with the first glimpse of his new home. "We . . . walked a short distance over our land and enjoyed the splendid sight—it is beautiful beyond expectation," he reported. "Excellent timber, good soil, many fine springs and a stream filled with fish. Water sufficient therein the whole year to drive a mill or saw mill. Wild grapes in abundance. Much game . . . in short all that one could expect."[10]

John and Margaret Owen shared their optimism in a letter home to family members in Wales: "Tell everyone who inquires after us that we think the country will prove very agreeable to us. We are only sorry that we did not come earlier, but 'better late than never.'"[11] Johann Schroeder could not contain his emotions while writing his first letter back to Germany in 1846. "Dear God, what I could tell you if I had only a half hour with you! You would marvel at it. I have seen much, I have become impressed with the might of God. . . . My eyes are filled with tears when I think that you still languish under the yoke."[12]

Water sources and soil quality were evaluated with care. "Now back to . . . daily trips to look at farms in which I found considerable differences in locations and soil," wrote John Kerler to a cousin in Germany in 1849. "Also, there was a great deal of difference in prices if the location [was] near or far from the city, or if the soil is good black earth, or clay or sandy."[13] Many of Wisconsin's early European immigrants had left landscapes almost completely devoid of timber. People who'd crept fearfully onto landowners' estates on moonless nights to poach twigs now wanted wooded land—or best of all, a mixture of forest and prairie. They were willing to confront the daunting struggle to clear timber if it meant having wood for building, for fuel, for fences, for market.

Yankee settlers were more likely to look favorably on open prairie land. Men imagined rippling fields of grain replacing waving wild grasses and flowers. They planned cash crops of rye, oats, and especially wheat, which was lucrative until the chinch bug and loss of soil fertility led to declining yields during the Civil War. The most profit-minded figured that when earnings declined, they could always sell out and move on. Their European neighbors watched this approach with bewilderment or disdain. "That is the way the Yankees do it," Henry Frank wrote home to his parents in Germany in 1857. "They bleed a good land dry, and when the yeast is removed, they sell, move on and buy the acre for 10 shillings ($1.25). They get rich doing that."[14] Echoed Eberhard Pflaume, who farmed in Manitowoc County for twelve years, "Americans must come to appreciate fertilization, crop rotation, and remaining in one location."[15]

Whatever their philosophy, whether European, British, or Yankee, the early settlers surely knew it would not be easy to create a new home. "Everyone that starts on the journey must consider that one must first taste sour before he can drink sweet," cautioned one immigrant, who'd been beckoned to the Upper Midwest by reports of shoulder-high grass and "many other glorious things."[16] The newcomers were lucky if they could obtain land; for most, hiring extra help or purchasing modern machinery was unthinkable. "At the very start of opening a farm . . . two implements were very necessary, in fact indispensable, viz: a plow and ax," recalled a Sauk Prairie pioneer. "Without the plow no farming could be done and, lacking an ax, no buildings or fences could be built."[17]

Even with a few more hand tools, years of labor stood between the immigrants' arrival and the farm of their dreams. "Some of the farm was wooded, but it was expected that in due time this would be grubbed to make farm land," noted Oscar Hallam, son of English immigrants. "I said 'grubbed' not 'cut,' that was the proper way to clear land."[18] Clearing timber with grub hoe, ax, and mattock was a sweat-soaked, back-aching, hands-rubbed-raw job.

Some of those who eagerly paced out the borders of their land had never held a hoe or scythe, but still felt the pull of an agrarian life. A Dutch miller and his wife would likely have starved had neighbors not shown them how to clear land and plant crops. German scholars and tradesmen who fled midcentury political upheaval and made their way to rural Wisconsin were known as "Latin farmers." Their complete lack of practical experience had results ranging from comical to disastrous.

For some pioneers, isolation, loneliness, and homesickness were more daunting than towering oak trees, bears in the hog pen, or getting the knack of tying scraggly sheaves of oats with only pieces of straw. Emeline Moulton poured out her anguish in a letter: "You don't know Aunt Dalinda how anxious I am to go back to Dear Old Vermont, and have a good visit with you all. . . . Should we never

*An ax was indispensable for anyone creating a new life in Wisconsin. Many new arrivals survived their first year or so by chopping firewood to sell or trade for supplies.* (WHI IMAGE ID 81388)

have the pleasure of meeting again on earth, let us anticipate a joyful meeting in Heaven where parting shall be known no more."[19] A woman from New York also acknowledged her sense of loss. "We have got forty acres deeded and when we get a house which I think will be before many years and if some of my folk were here I should be considerable well contented," Orpha Ranney wrote. "But as long as I remain here alive I shall be subject to homesick fits."[20]

Counterbalancing despair was a pervasive spirit of cooperation in rural settlements that helped many pioneers survive that often-brutal first year. "Almost everybody needed some kind of helping out," recalled a black woman who lived in the integrated rural community of Pleasant Ridge.[21] Immigrants in lonely valleys and tiny communities watched for the next crop of newcomers. Women sought the company of other women; even if they didn't speak the same language, a shared cup of tea and wordless but palpable empathy provided comfort. "In the

*Loneliness was a challenge on the frontier, particularly for pioneer women, who had fewer opportunities than men to leave the homestead.* (WHI IMAGE ID 3187)

early days the latch-string was always out in a hearty welcome," Caroline Alter recalled. "Many articles of food were hard to get and if anyone had an extra supply of something good he divided it with his neighbor."[22]

Not everyone—or every dream—survived. Theodore Rodolf of Switzerland arrived in 1832. After obtaining land from the government, he and a friend "returned home proud and happy in the thought that we had now again a home of our own. But we did not enjoy that home very long. Our experiment in farming did not result in success."[23] Gustaf Unonius came in 1841 with visions of establishing a Swedish settlement in Wisconsin, and his letters sparked many Scandinavians to pack their trunks. He wrote of the settlement at Pine Lake:

> Wisconsin Territory, where we have settled, is for the present considered to be the most favorable region in the United States for colonization. The country is beautiful, adorned with oak woods and prairies broken by rivers and lakes swarming with fish; in addition it is one of the healthiest areas in America. . . . We have taken 160 acres in a section located twenty-nine miles from Milwaukee. We are the first settlers here. We have deliberately chosen this section in the hope that a number of our countrymen will join us. The location is one of the most beautiful imaginable. On the map in the land office it has already been designated "New Upsala." What dear memories are aroused by this name![24]

A decade later Swedish writer Frederika Bremer toured the area. "We rowed along the wooded shores," she wrote. "And here, upon a lofty promontory covered with splendid masses of wood, was New Upsala to stand—such was the intention of Unonius and his friends. . . . Ah! That wild district will not maintain Upsala's sons. I saw the desolate houses where [they] struggled in vain to live."[25]

Still, many settlers *did* manage—with what Oscar Hallam summarized as "hard work, indomitable pluck, and a rigid economy"—to create farms and provide for their children. Hallam also described the essential need to understand the land, the climate, the turning seasons. "[My parents] planned and they executed," he explained. "They planted in early spring, they cultivated diligently in the summer.

They garnered and threshed at proper times in summer and fall. They plowed and fertilized in the fall, for the next year's crop. They greased harness on rainy days. They chopped wood, shelled corn, and fanned grain on winter days."[26]

That intimacy with the landscape—and indomitable pluck—was ultimately found on thousands of farms throughout Wisconsin. There was no distinct "pioneer era"; while the earliest Yankee settlers in the state's southeast corner were looking with pride at decades of work and accomplishment, later arrivals were entering a pioneer period of their own in the rugged cutover land in northern Wisconsin. But John Kerler spoke for many of those who sacrificed and planned and stuck it out through hard times. "Of all my former occupations, there was

*This family proudly posed for the photographer in an image composed to show all they had managed to acquire in Wisconsin: a fine frame house, large outbuildings, store-bought furniture and china. A copy may have been sent across the Atlantic to loved ones in the Old Country—proof that the immigrants were not merely surviving, but thriving.* (WHI IMAGE ID 26722)

none that appealed to me as agriculture does, and to this I am now devoted with all my soul," he wrote in 1853. "What I formerly often wished for in sad hours, I have found here."[27] He, and others from Russia and Belgium, Pennsylvania and Massachusetts, Finland and Scotland and so many other places, knew that they were, at last, *home*.

◆—•—◆

The experiences of the women, children, and men who settled Wisconsin linger in more than their diaries and letters. Intangibles are found in their descendants' unique cultural identity, work ethic, or spirit of resiliency. Individuals and

*This photograph was taken at an angle that included the farm's original log cabin, later dwarfed by the large frame home. Perhaps the original immigrants were among the people pictured celebrating a wedding in 1890, parents or grandparents of the bride and groom.* (WHI IMAGE ID 1522)

communities also treasure tangible links to the past: battered immigrant trunks and faded photographs, heirloom tomato seeds and old-breed sheep, recipes for lefse and pierogies and snickerdoodles.

More stories are preserved in the beams and boards of the buildings constructed by Wisconsin's pioneers. A few lucky families still claim proud ownership of the farms first tilled by their ancestors a century or more ago. Some log cabins are hidden beneath aluminum siding; some still stand lopsided beside new pole barns. But by the middle of the twentieth century, many structures were disintegrating beyond salvage or had been bulldozed to make room for new buildings.

Fortunately, a visionary group of historians and landscape architects took action and created a safe haven: Old World Wisconsin. This outdoor ethnic museum sprawls over 576 acres of land within the Kettle Moraine State Forest—the largest outdoor museum of rural life in the United States. More than sixty structures have been moved and fully restored, including ten working farms and a crossroads village. Their stories are shared with guests by interpreters wearing period clothing.

But Old World Wisconsin is about more than the families and cultural groups that are literally represented by logs and bricks and mortar. Collectively, the historic site tells the broader story of people looking for, working for, and ultimately creating new homes in a new land. And that's a story with relevance for almost everyone.

I first visited Old World Wisconsin in 1981, when the site was only six years old. I have no family roots in Wisconsin, and my own ethnic heritage is not reflected in any of the homes or buildings restored at the site. But there were stories here for me, too. That visit compelled me to join the continuum of people who have left the East Coast and settled in the state.

After two years as an interpreter, I moved behind the scenes and served as curator of interpretation and collections. But my fondest memories are of the time spent working on the farms, experiencing the changing seasons in a sensory and visceral way. Because Old World Wisconsin is a living museum, interpreters learn experientially by re-creating as best they can the natural rhythms of nineteenth-century rural life.

Visitors experience those cycles as well, of course, but only to the extent that their time permits. Most catch only a glimpse during infrequent visits . . . until now. Loyd Heath, who's been roaming the site with camera in hand for years, has managed to capture the essence of this living historic site as it changes day by day, month by month. His images—with the contributions of a few other talented photographers—evoke immigrant life in lush detail. As you turn the pages, you will almost smell rhubarb pie baking, almost feel sweat dampening your shirt, almost hear a farmer calling to his oxen. The photographs may well provoke a new curiosity about your family stories, about your ancestors' search for a new home.

Warm thanks to the many interpreters and volunteers who provide guests a glimpse of life in an earlier time. And this book would not have been possible without the work of Marty Perkins, who did more to develop and shape the historic site than anyone else. Marty began his career in 1976 by helping to identify, dismantle, and restore historic structures; for many years he served as curator of interpretation and research. I offer *A Settler's Year* in quiet tribute to his legacy at Old World Wisconsin.

—Kathleen Ernst

# SPRING

"The sun rose about half-past six this morning sending its silvery rays over the land to reveal nature in all her beauty. How pleasant the warmth of spring is after the cold of winter! Everything seems to have regained its liberty. The birds twitter in the trees, the hens cackle, and the deer leap and gallop over the fields and plains as if to give expression to that liberty and equality which reign in the land of freedom. Where are they to be found in Europe?"
*(Søren Bache Diary, March 1, 1845)*

Lengthening days heartened settlers weary of winter's brittle cold. Icicles began to drip. Thrushes and wrens began to sing, and spring peepers formed a bell-like chorus. The primordial cries of sandhill cranes drifted from the marshes. Hazelnut trees glowed pale green and yellow with tiny leaves and flowers, and clusters of white blossoms misted the chokecherries. Hard-packed snow turned to slush, then squelching mud, and men removed sleigh runners from their wagon boxes. For newcomers, everything was new—terrain, native flowers and herbs, migrating birds. Each day brought more discoveries.

In the early years of settlement, when provisions ran low and harvest was long months away, spring was only a promise of better times. Women craving fresh greens foraged for nettles and cow cabbage to boil, and brewed a spring tonic from goldenseal and sarsaparilla roots dug in the woods. Pioneers trudged to the nearest crossroads village for vital supplies. A young Belgian woman in Kewaunee County left home long before dawn with a sixty-pound sack of wheat on her back and made a fifteen-hour, thirty-mile trudge to the nearest mill. After sleeping at the mill, she returned home the next day with the precious flour. "It was considered a vacation of a sort," wrote her son. "It was a change of motion!"[1]

With basic necessities attended to, men who'd arrived the previous autumn strode over their land, getting acquainted with it, estimating how much seed wheat they needed and calculating corn yields. When frost left the soil, they attacked it with heavy grub hoes. Women planted potatoes and corn between the roots of trees girdled and dying slowly in what would one day be fields.

When they could afford it—which sometimes took years—immigrants bought oxen and scouring plows designed to slice the prairie's deep, dense mat of rooted plants. The sod turned with a reluctant tearing sound as stumbling men fought to maintain straight furrows. Neighbors worked cooperatively, sometimes hitching five or six teams of oxen to a single plow. Cultivating among tree stumps was equally difficult; elastic roots often whipped the plower's legs.

Managing oxen required clever thinking as well as brawn, for the lumbering animals sometimes had minds of their own. Boys yelled themselves hoarse in Polish, in Swedish, in Scottish brogues. Men who'd labored only as shoemakers, shepherds, or store clerks needed tutelage from neighbors. Too often they watched with despair as their yoke ran away. Finding the animals usually involved slogging through wiry prairie grass or shoulder-high slough hay, plunging into unseen pools, and success attained only long after dark.

Kind women carried chicks in their aprons as a gift to new-come neighbors. Men with a few coins to spare walked home from the closest market with an indignant piglet or two wriggling in a grain sack carried over one shoulder. European immigrants made the welfare of whatever livestock they could afford a particular priority, even if that meant constructing a stable before building a cabin, or—if the family had a cabin—establishing a temporary animal pen inside. Some Yankees thought that odd, but people who had staked *everything* on starting fresh in Wisconsin could not afford to lose a single hen or hog.

Cows, too, were purchased as soon as finances allowed. In springtime heifers freshened, calves bawled, and meals again included milk, butter, and cheese. Cows roamed freely in warm weather, foraging in nearby woods or prairies, returning home only to be milked or fed a bit of salt twice a day. Children were responsible for keeping cattle—and deer—from gardens and fields. As the daughter of one German settler wryly noted, "Children were much cheaper than fences."[2] Even after fences were erected, boys and girls spent hours chasing enormous clouds of pigeons from just-planted fields.

Children often shouldered adult responsibility at an early age, but they found their own fun as well. When the maple sap ran, smoke drifted from "sugar kettles," and boys and girls begged for a taste of sweet golden syrup. They shed shoes as soon as possible and delighted in the wet, dank smell of thawing earth. "Often in early spring, on sunny days, we would go in swimming in [nearby] ponds while big cakes of ice were floating in the water," recalled Uriah S. Hollister, "but we were not obliged to do it and it was great fun."[3]

Bachelors, wives, and children established robust kitchen gardens. Europeans retrieved the seeds that, months earlier, they'd tucked into twists of paper and nestled reverently into their immigrant trunks. After crossing the Atlantic, those tiny kernels promised a taste of the Old Country.

Yankees who'd transported precious lilac or rose bushes patted them into Wisconsin soil. Potted plants, too, received gentle care. "My house plants were pretty well smashed up when I got here," one woman wrote home. "I have set them out and they begin to revive some. I have not seen any flowers as nice as mother's since I left home."[4] Other women sprinkled hollyhock and marigold seeds beneath their windows, transplanted wild lupines by their front doors, or trained honeysuckle to grow around cabin windows.

The frenzied labor of creating farms from prairie and forest faded as years passed, giving way to the urge to improve them. Instead of dragging branches to brush piles while their fathers girdled ancient oaks, children picked frost-shoved stones from fields. Women smiled as the perennials they'd coddled from seeds grew lush and shrubby. European men, with an eye to their descendants' future, developed complex schemes of crop rotation. Horses replaced oxen as New England farmers brought favorite teams to the Upper Midwest and began breeding programs. Yankees also established farmers' clubs and scheduled educational lectures and demonstrations to help everyone keep up with the latest trends and innovations.

Prosperity also allowed families to acquire what one settler called "that supreme luxury, a flock of sheep."[5] On one of the year's first warm days, boys drove bleating sheep to nearby ponds and creeks to wash. Farmers needed skill to shear fleece away from their animals in a single piece—especially if their animals were wrinkly-skinned Merinos, prized for their lustrous wool. After shearing, women bundled the fleeces to clean and spin as time permitted, never wasting a moment with idle hands. "[My great-grandmother] raised her own sheep and spun her own wool," one woman recalled. "When it was necessary to go to the store, she walked along the road, barefooted, knitting all the way and stopping on the edge of town to put on her shoes. She carried her shoes in a basket on her arm. After her purchases were made she again took off her shoes and walked, knitting all the while, back home."[6]

With sunshine warming their shoulders, immigrants began or continued the work of creating their new homes. "It took courage to plant a settlement," noted one descendant, "and the women were indeed brave to face such a wilderness."[7] But with breaking plows and red geraniums, the settlers *did* face that challenge. They dreamed of abundance despite quivering muscles, blistered palms, and homesick hearts. When spring softened the landscape, all things seemed possible.

Nature provided a glorious spectacle for people weary of snow and ice. Settlers reveled in the new green of spring, reflected here in a kettle pond.

The primordial calls of returning sandhill cranes echoed from marshes and meadows—and sometimes from pastures as well.

Newcomers desperate to turn soil and plant a few crops began clearing land as soon as conditions permitted. Sometimes improving their living quarters had to be postponed. "This was real pioneer life," one man remembered. "No fire place or chimney, no stove of course. Mother did all the cooking out of doors, a frying pan, tea kettle and baking kettle were the only conveniences." (Uriah S. Hollister, *Letter and Reminiscences, 1839 and ca. 1912*)

"From 1838 to 1840 we saw some pretty close times. . . . We caught suckers and red-horse in the Bark river, boiled them into a sort of porridge, and ate them with nothing but salt. After a few such meals with nothing else, I was not particularly fond of fresh fish." (E. G. Fifield, *Janesville Gazette,* June 24, 1886)

Baking was a huge chore for women who had to grind grain by hand. "Corn was ground in a hand mill," one woman recalled. "Peas were roasted, ground and used as coffee, and it had a bitter taste." (Margaretha Schwalbach, quoted in Nick Bruehl, *Chilton Times,* February 8, 1930)

Warm weather allowed settlers to move some chores outside—a welcome change for those who'd spent long months jammed into small cabins. Bachelors might tackle their own laundry, or—if they were lucky—they might swap labor or game for domestic chores with a neighbor.

Women on the frontier of white settlement were accustomed to doing heavy chores. After cutting wood or working a grub hoe all day, they wearily began house chores when the sun set.

Children began assuming responsibilities, such as fetching water, collecting wood chips, and picking stones from fields, at an early age.

For a newly arrived family, a pig was a crucial investment. Old breeds, such as these Tamworth pigs, were generally tough and self-sufficient.

However, a temporary pen built inside the cabin would protect precious piglets from any late snowstorms.

Women dreaming of eggs and chicken stew were also eager to obtain chicks.

This "stovewood" building, home to elderly Polish immigrants, conveniently featured a chicken coop and living quarters under one roof.

The stovewood style of construction does not reflect a particular ethnic group but was a relatively quick and easy way to build a sturdy structure.

"The Americans leave their cattle out in the open, summer and winter, so that the milk often is frozen in the udder. I could not bring myself to do that, so that the cattle barn was first to be erected." (Dr. Louis Frank, *The Frank-Kerler Letters, 1849–1864*)

Immigrants who'd left areas where timber was scarce brought a preservation ethic to Wisconsin. This half-timbered stable was used by a Pomeranian family. It also featured a roof thatched with rye straw, as did the large grain barn on the left.

The half-timbered house featured only a cooking niche . . .

. . . and an enlarged central chimney called a *Schwarze Kuche*, or black kitchen. The central fire pit allowed women to cook and smoke meat on poles overhead at the same time. Coals left from heating the bake oven were also raked into the pit, ensuring that no fuel was wasted.

Those who could afford a team of oxen had an enormous advantage as the work to create a farm began. "When emigrants came trekking in with the covered wagons to settle on the land, it was Buck and Bright who toted them in and did the heavy work around the homestead after they finally got settled," noted one man. "They helped clear the land, did the breaking and plowing, hauled the grain to market, and was [*sic*] the general handy vehicle around the place." (Pat Collins, *Antigo Daily Journal,* April 2, 1930)

Families wrestling fields from wooded land faced grueling labor. The first year, they girdled trees and planted around them. As trees died and time permitted, fields were improved. Finally only stumps remained to be heaved from the earth with chains, crowbars, and straining teams of oxen.

In spring European immigrants fetched precious seeds from their trunks. Men planted as they'd been taught in the Old World, and women planned familiar meals for their families. "We are introducing German vegetables little by little," one woman wrote, "while the American lives on cake, meat, and potatoes all year." (Dr. Louis Frank, *The Frank-Kerler Letters, 1849–1864*)

"Gardening is as eminently the branch of horticulture for May as tree-planting for April, and should more or less engross the attention of all who have any ground to cultivate."
(*The Wisconsin Farmer and Northwest Cultivator,* May 1858)

Many Yankees, however, created elaborate gardens that produced a diverse abundance of fruits and vegetables.

Settlers craving a taste of something green eagerly harvested the first spears of asparagus.

Pie plant (rhubarb) was welcomed as another source of fresh food in early spring, sweetened with honey or maple syrup if sugar was too dear.

Struggling families who'd arrived with nothing considered the purchase of a cow a joyful achievement.

Until fences could be built, however, owning a cow meant chasing a cow. "My first bossy I will always remember, especially when it came to milking time," wrote one pioneer. "This cow had a vast territory for pasture, consisting of cranberry swamps, wild meadows, etc., and I would have to start out right after dinner looking for her in order to find her in time for milking that evening." ( Joseph Anderson, in "Pioneering in Early Days," *Washburn Times,* February 22, 1923)

Although well-to-do Yankee ladies left barn work to the men, most newly arrived European women took responsibility for dairy chores.

The addition of sheep on an immigrant's farm was another sign of success.

During spring lambing season, farmers spent many nights in the barn, making sure that all was well.

Shearing commenced when the weather was warm enough to safely relieve sheep of their heavy coats. The job required a strong back and sharp shears. The most adept men could shear a sheep in under a minute.

Colorful hoods and shawls,
hanging above baskets of
American wool, evoked
memories of Norway.

Children began learning how to card wool at an early age, and to knit as well. "I can't remember when I learned to knit," remembered one woman. "It seemed to me that I always knew how." (Angela Haste Favell, *Milwaukee Journal*, August 7, 1932)

After enough wool was carded, a woman might move her spinning wheel to the front porch on a fine day. But many children drifted to sleep to the musical *whir* of a spinning wheel, and travelers often heard the humming sound as they passed cabins at night.

An early settler recalled, "Many times did I hold the skein with hands and arms outstretched and swinging back and forth in order to release the yarn between the thumb and finger, first of one hand and then of the other, as my mother or one of my sisters wound the skein into balls." (Channing Mather, *Sheboygan Press,* May 11, 1929)

Immigrants were usually so busy that mittens, blankets, and shawls knit or woven in the New World were plain and functional . . .

. . . but if time permitted, women prepared natural dyes from onion skins, walnuts, elderberries, yarrow, or other materials gathered from garden, woods, or prairie. Dyeing some skeins let them look forward to knitting or weaving more colorful pieces.

Newcomers may have attended their first worship services in drafty cabins, but pioneers built hundreds of small churches before Wisconsin achieved statehood. Those who had fled Europe because of religious persecution rejoiced in their ability to establish a new church in the New World. Isolated settlers waited eagerly for spring, when weather permitted travel to church. Some rose before dawn in order to arrive before services started. In the years when livestock roamed free, worshippers sometimes heard pigs rooting beneath the floor of chapels built on blocks.

The original Pleasant Ridge church stood on a hill, beckoning area residents.

Polish immigrants in rural areas often erected roadside shrines, as they had in the Old World. A strong faith helped many immigrants, Yankee and European alike, face the challenges of starting over in a new place.

# SUMMER

"As concerns the weather, there has been an excessive
amount of rain and thunder this spring and summer,
so no one can remember the like of it. Likewise, the heat
was so intense the last part of June, that it was almost
impossible to work at all. If we sat down in the shade,
the sweat drops ran off our clothes like hail, and we had
to change shirts two and three times each day."
*(Anders Jensen Stortroen, 1858)*

Wild roses and coneflowers bloomed, painted turtles crawled from their eggs, and sulphur butterflies flitted through clearings. The farm families had done what they could: newcomers soberly dropping single seeds into holes scratched among stumps, the more settled mechanically sowing freshly harrowed acres from a horse-drawn seeder. Now men eyed the sky, hoping for just enough rain, no more. Women checked garden plots for both tender new growth and any sign of pest. Crop success now depended largely on forces of nature beyond their control.

Making hay filled many of the year's longest days. Pioneers lucky enough to own livestock found native prairie and marsh grasses theirs to harvest. Cutting that heavy crop with sickle or scythe left men bone-weary. Still, the abundance was almost overwhelming for immigrants who'd left exhausted land behind. "Almost everywhere the grass was so thick and high that a skilled man, without working too hard, could cut between ten and fifteen *skippund* a day," wrote Søren Bache—an impressive harvest. Due to inexperience and intense heat, Bache did not do as well. Still, he and a companion cut enough hay in two weeks to see five cows and one horse through the coming winter.[1]

Women and children raked the hay from stumps and fence corners, careful not to catch and break hand-carved tines. Once the grass was dry, they formed it into cocks, and later hauled it to storage shed or barn. Women helped load and unload wagons—a job that required skill to do well. A good loader knew how to pile hay efficiently, arranged just so to facilitate the ultimate pitching, forkful by forkful, from wagon to haymow.

Grains were also of vital importance. "What would we not give for our ordinary barley-groats and cut barley!" one early immigrant lamented. "The Americans do not know how to grind grain, and our Swedish stomachs sigh in vain for our beloved porridge."[2] Most farmers planted rye and oats for home use, but long before Wisconsin's dairy industry emerged, wheat was literally a golden crop. In the first years of white settlement, farmers doggedly ploughed under thousands of prairie acres and sowed them with wheat.

No harvest, perhaps, was eyed with such worried scrutiny. "The prompt and timely gathering of the wheat crop, when at just the right stage of ripeness and maturity, is a matter of the first importance," noted the editors of *The Wisconsin Farmer and Northwest Cultivator*.[3] It would not do to harvest grain before the kernels were plump. But if rain didn't come before harvest, seeds would scorch and wither beneath the merciless sun; a single severe storm might destroy a year's crop. Farmers walked through rippling seas of tawny grain pinching seeds between thumb and forefinger, sniffing the air for hint of violent weather, hoping that *this* year, God or fate would provide perfect conditions for harvest.

Most settlers considered the cradle scythe the implement of choice. Skilled gleaners moved with a swinging, rhythmic grace. The best men could cut four acres a day, but that took practice: "When I first began to cradle wheat I thought my ribs should break the next morning when I started in again," recalled Frederick Honajager, a Prussian immigrant who arrived in 1854.[4] Long blades cut stalks with a *wish-wish* sound from dawn until dusk, while the cradles collected and dropped them in tidy rows for the binders coming along behind. Cut grain had to be raked and bound into bundles, shocked, and stacked by hand.

"I have raked [cut grain] many a day," recalled Celina Peckham Wood, who helped harvest during the Civil War. "I could bind a bundle, but not very quick, so they kept me raking."[5] But many women were accustomed to field labor. "My mother worked on the Johnston farm, shearing sheep, binding in the field, etc.," wrote Honajager. "She surely could work, and when she beat Sam Nelson, crack wheat binder of the neighborhood, Johnston gave him the laugh."[6] Another pioneer noted, "Mrs. Nass has always been a persistent worker in the fields. . . . Her husband cradled the grain and she bound it. . . . When she could not do her housework in the day time because of the press of outside duties, she did it at night after supper and the chores were done."[7] Mrs. Nass, who'd been ten when her family left Prussia, also raised eighteen children.

As time passed and purses permitted, agricultural innovations eased the demands of such physical labor and made it possible to expand farms. Horse-drawn reapers and self-binders displaced many of the itinerant harvest hands who'd earned a dollar a day for swinging a cradle scythe. "America is an inventive land," Johann Schroeder wrote home. "Here are machines for cutting grain, for threshing, for cleaning, for sacking."[8]

Animal-powered threshing machines greatly expedited the work. Uriah Hollister remembered one early model: "It had no fanning mill attachment, the grain and chaff all came out together; but it beat the flail out of sight and was popular until something better came on the market."[9] Progressive farmers congregated at agricultural exhibitions to study mechanical innovations and purebred livestock. "There were horses such as one could not find at the October festival in Munich," John Kerler marveled in 1853. "Sheep-raising was no less represented."[10] While men debated the merits of French Merino rams, women gathered in separate tents to watch demonstrations of foot-powered sewing machines and other domestic wonders.

Yankee settlers brought their belief in the necessity of an engaged citizenship with them, even if in the early years many wealthy white farmers believed in limiting voting privileges. Independence Day celebrations were eagerly anticipated. Children fidgeted beneath the sun while town dignitaries pontificated, but they shrieked with excitement when older boys lit turpentine-soaked rag balls on fire and tossed them into the air. Blacksmiths stacked one anvil on top of another with a layer of gunpowder between, lit a fuse, and ran. Moments later, with a satisfying explosion, the top anvil flew thirty or forty feet into the air.

Children often attended school in the summer, for it was easier to spare them from home during the hottest months than during planting or final harvest time. Still, despite lessons and chores, children vividly recalled turning farmwork into play. They played hide-and-seek among towering straw stacks. They built dams in creeks to create swimming pools, and searched for clams, fish, crawfish, and pretty pebbles. When sent to gather wild raspberries or dewberries, they came home with fruit-smeared fingers and bellies as full as their buckets.

As summer's sticky heat faded, women and men took stock. They'd likely suffered from dense clouds of mosquitoes and gnats, and battled seed-stealing gophers and blackbirds. Prairie fires may have consumed haystacks and drought may have shriveled crops. Some dreams had been shattered by hail, by chinch bugs in the grain and caterpillars in the cabbage, by the limits of even a strong man's ability or a hardy woman's determination.

Other dreams literally bore fruit, as evidenced by washtubs of beans and crocks of pickled cucumbers and barns filled to the rafters with hay and straw. "My farm is thriving," John Kerler wrote home to Germany in 1852. "In addition to God's blessing, our work has not been in vain."[11]

Spring's mercurial days of promise inevitably flowed into the long, hot weeks of summer. The season brought new wonders for Wisconsin's early settlers, including blazing star and other lush prairie flowers. "The whole country-side was abloom with the most gorgeous wild flowers," recalled Ingeborg Holdahl Alvstad. "We children picked them by the handful and there was always more." (Ingeborg Holdahl Alvstad, *Reminiscences—Pioneer Days in Wisconsin*)

New arrivals created farms with little more than determination, hand tools, and oxen. But as years went by, agricultural innovations such as cultivators became available—and affordable. Subsistence farmers began to dream of raising cash crops.

Women benefited from new machinery, too. A sheep-powered treadmill attached to a butter churn or washing machine worked efficiently.

Once gardens began to produce, women and children spent long hours inspecting cabbage for worms, pulling weeds from flower beds, and harvesting the food that would see them through the year.

Flax was a labor-intensive but important crop. Once mature, the plants were pulled and the seed heads were threshed from the stalks.

After a drying process, women crushed stalks in a flax brake (left), then held them against a board (center) and scraped away bits of stalk with a wooden knife. Only then could they begin to clean the inner fibers.

Hackles like this one were used to comb out flax fibers.

Hackling left women with smooth fibers to spin into linen thread. They saved the tangles of coarser fibers left in the hackle, called tow, to spin into twine.

Once a quantity of fibers had been cleaned, it was "fit for the spinning of the family linens, homespuns, many pieces of clothing and tablecloths," recalled Margaretha Schwalbach. (Nick Bruehl, *Chilton Times*, February 8, 1930)

Digging baby potatoes in August was especially rewarding for girls who'd spent
sticky June days scraping potato beetle larvae from young plants.

The first harvest meant roasted or boiled potatoes for supper, and the promise of full bins to last through the winter.

Before the Civil War, women preserved eggs as best they could by covering them with sawdust.

"Eggs were 5 cents a dozen; we thought it wouldn't pay to sell them, so thought we would eat them, and we had fried eggs, boiled eggs, baked eggs and eggs in every conceivable form, but the hens were ambitious and we couldn't near keep up with them, so we sold 9 dozen to a neighbor for the magnificent sum of 40 cents, and considered ourselves fortunate to receive the cash for them."
(Mrs. Hannah Parker, 1857; *Wautoma Argus*, February 13, 1924)

Once canning jars became available, women had an easier time preserving food.
Jars also provided airtight and mouse-proof containers for dried foods.

Settlers knew they would crave fruit during the coming winter, and they preserved as much as they could. Women kept a vigilant eye on precious grape crops, dropping pests into basins of kerosene. They also foraged for additional harvests. "We had some busy weeks gathering and canning hundreds of quarts of wild raspberries, blackberries, dewberries and goose berries," wrote one woman. "This country treats you well even in its wildest state." (Mrs. L. N. Ferguson, *Marinette Eagle-Star*, April 4, 1916)

If a boy's fishing excursion was particularly successful, a family could enjoy
the bounty fresh and dried. A Finnish sauna, usually used for bathing,
made a fine place for smoking fish.

It was difficult to leave the farm during the growing season, but sometimes the services provided in small villages made the trip necessary. By summer's end, prosperous farmers were also bringing excess crops to sell or trade.

A broken implement might prompt an emergency trip to the blacksmith's shop. The smith could also shoe oxen and horses.

Careful men soaked their wheels to prevent the wood from drying and coming apart. If a wheel needed major repair or replacement, however, farmers turned to skilled wagon makers.

The shoemaker might entice passersby with a display of the latest style in boots . . .

. . . but most farm families relied on the plain but sturdy shoes he made. Many pioneers, especially children, went barefoot in warm weather to preserve their shoes.

Yankee settlers, steeped in New England's political heritage, brought the gift of democracy to the heartland. Rural families often traveled long distances to hear speakers and participate in meetings.

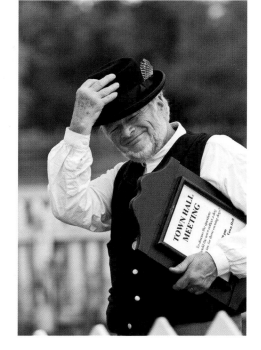

While official topics were formally debated at the Town Hall . . .

. . . village shops provided
informal gathering spots for
the exchange of news . . .

. . . and spirited discussion.

Summer terms brought children tramping from their farms to the nearest school.

Some of the earliest accounts of one-room schools recall students openly challenging their teachers, a problem resolved only with whipping or other forms of physical authority. However, most students fondly remembered the instructors who managed to teach multiple grades at once—and often had fun with the students as well.

In early, isolated settlements, teachers sometimes conducted lessons in Norwegian or German or Swedish. Later, some children of foreign-born immigrants heard English spoken for the first time when they started school.

Although there were moments of frustration, most graduates of one-room schools agreed that sharing a class with older students, and hearing their lessons recited, helped their own progress.

By late summer, fields of grain rippled green, and then golden, in the sunshine. Such luxuriant crops astonished European immigrants used to coaxing scanty yields from worn soil. "Oh my dear cousin and brothers," wrote one man, "I wish you had all been here in the harvest time, so that you could have seen the lovely grains. You would never have wanted to return to Germany." (Johann Schroeder letter, December 1846)

As yields increased, neighbors exchanged work at threshing time. Even a progressive farmer with a horse-powered rig appreciated extra help bringing grain from the field, feeding the threshing machine, and hauling grain and straw.

A line of horses hitched to a fence provided testimony to the community spirit. "Threshing time was fun time," recalled one early settler who as a child had delighted in the work parties. "The neighbors started coming very early to eat breakfast before going to work." (Ingeborg Holdahl Alvstad, *Reminiscences— Pioneer Days in Wisconsin*)

Women anxiously began baking for the threshing crew well in advance. A brick bake oven, like the one in the wall behind the cookstove in this summer kitchen, could hold a dozen loaves at once. The long wooden paddle propped in the corner was used to handle the loaves. Proud cooks relied on favorite recipes, knowing the crew would sample—and compare—meals at every farm in the neighborhood.

"The men came in with a rush, and took seats wherever they could find them, and their attack on the boiled potatoes and chicken should have been appalling to the women, but it was not. They enjoyed seeing them eat." (Hamlin Garland, *A Son of the Middle Border*)

Farmwives were grateful for help, as they might be responsible for feeding a threshing crew breakfast, a midmorning lunch, dinner, and a late-afternoon meal.

Exhausted cooks and field hands often ate in silence . . .

. . . but the shared meals had a social element, too.

Children were kept busy washing dishes, carrying snacks and water to the crew in the field, tending to oxen and horses . . . and perhaps dreaming of working their own farm one day.

# AUTUMN

"I wandered along the road; the country, glowing with
sunshine, opened before me like an immense English
park, with a background of the most beautiful arable land,
fringed with leafy woods, now splendid with the colors of
autumn. Here and there I saw little farm-houses, built on
the skirts of the forest, mostly of log-houses; occasionally,
however, might be seen a frame house, as well as small gray
stone cottages. I saw the people out in the fields busied
with their corn-harvest. I addressed them in Norwegian,
and they joyfully fell into conversation."
*(Fredrika Bremer, October 5, 1850)*

Days inexorably grew shorter. Prairies shimmered with goldenrod and purple asters. Maples flamed yellow, sumac glowed ruby-red, and golden light slanted through the trees. Wood ducks and white-throated sparrows migrated south. Women pulled wool shawls from trunks, and children reluctantly retrieved the shoes they'd kicked under the bed in spring. Crickets serenaded as harvest continued.

In the early years of settlement, families worked through the fall to thresh wheat and rye and oats. Men without barn floors spread sheets or canvas tarps; one made a threshing floor "of blue clay baked in the sun."[1] Farmers fashioned flails from stout oak sticks. Fathers and sons circled bundles of grain placed on the threshing floor, beating kernels from the stalks. Other men drove oxen in endless rounds to trample the kernels free.

Then came the winnowing. "A couple of sheets were spread upon the ground to catch the grain," one man explained, "and with a tin pan for a half bushel and the gentle breezes of nature for his fanning mill," the pioneers winnowed their wheat.[2] On still days, children waved pieces of bark—not too hard, just so—until their arms ached. Women knelt on the sheet for hours, carefully picking out bits of chaff.

Threshing provided clean bedding for livestock—and for people who slept on straw-stuffed mattresses, too. "What fun we children had," recalled Ingeborg Holdahl Alvstad. "We were allowed to do the stuffing after emptying the old straw."[3] This task took practice, and after children wrestled the ungainly straw ticks back onto their beds, mothers surreptitiously redistributed straw within the heavy cotton covers.

When the first frost rimed the grass, children also helped empty gardens—gathering vegetables that grew above ground before moving on to root crops. The vines twining among cornstalks sometimes bore magnificent pumpkins and squash. "[Our pumpkins] grow to weigh as much as 30 pounds," one German immigrant marveled. "My wife could not carry two of them at the same time, she had to come in with one. They are very valuable to make sirup [sic] out of and also for cattle, they make much milk."[4] Ellen Spaulding Miller also treasured her harvest, but worried about supplies: "We pay 35 cts for butter, 45 cts for Eggs, and I am afraid I shan't get enough to make my Pumpkin Pies for Christmas. I have got a glorious big Pumpkin in the cellar, to make pies of."[5]

Children hauled baskets of rutabagas and carrots to root cellars. Women tied muslin over crocks of pickled cucumbers, and braided onions to hang beneath the eaves. They sliced splendid piles of cabbage into big crocks, and boys and girls took turns banging the heavy tamp, releasing the juices for sauerkraut. Muddy heaps of turnips waited for attention in kitchen corners. Kitchens smelled of vinegar and damp earth.

Acres of whispering cornstalks prompted another labor-intensive harvest. Sweet corn was sliced from the cob, dried, and stored in sacks for the winter; once reconstituted, it made "very palatable food." Field corn was sometimes shelled, boiled in lye to loosen the hulls, and repeatedly rinsed. "It was then boiled until soft and eaten with milk, or fried in fat or with bits of bacon," wrote an early settler in Richland County. "It made rich, nutritious food."[6] New immigrants discovered that some established farmers needed help with the corn harvest; in 1867, some Czechoslovakian women earned twenty-five cents a day husking corn for "richer farmers" in the La Crosse area.[7] As years passed and communities grew, volunteer help could usually be purchased with the promise of a husking bee. On crisp moonlit evenings, unmarried young people husked corn until late at night, when the host and hostess provided cider and coffee, bread and cake and sausage. Tired workers perked up when fiddlers or an accordion player let loose with tunes from the Old Country. Aching hands didn't keep courting couples from dancing around blazing bonfires.

Potatoes were among the last vegetables harvested. Children turned each vine's hill carefully, for it wouldn't do to pierce any of the tubers. One immigrant recalled a "glorious brushwood fire" when his family celebrated the season with "a Harvest Home Supper and potato bake. . . . When the fire was almost burned to ashes, we put into the embers the freshly dug potatoes each wrapped in a thick coat of mud. No other baked potato can compare with such as we raised."[8]

Harvest suppers were only one of the late season's diversions. Settlers were generally quick to help their neighbors, but with the anxious frenzy of harvest past, many gatherings took on a distinctly social element. "Life was not so easy," recalled one woman, "but we always had time for old fashioned country pleasures. Many were the quilting bees and the paring bees and the raising bees that we had. We used to take our work and go and spend all day with a neighbor, and real sociable times we had."[9]

"Logging bees and raisings were held very frequently," echoed another pioneer, "and the people who attended always had a good time." The refreshments included "all the 'schnapps' that was good for a man who had to make his way home after dark through the woods. At night after a bee the men remain and all the neighborhood women came in and all danced till late at night."[10]

In very late autumn, when the maple leaves were brittle-brown and boys doing first morning chores left footsteps in heavy frost, families prepared for butchering. The squealing piglets carried home in sacks the previous spring now weighed over two hundred pounds. With luck, nearby oaks had produced an abundance of acorns; nothing was finer to fatten hogs. With a bit more luck, black bears would not raid the hog pen before butchering day. The truly fortunate families might spare an ox from their growing herd to butcher as well, and could anticipate both beef and pork in the coming months.

Hickory smoke wafted from the smokehouse and apple butter simmered on the stove. Settlers heard the faint cries of the last migrating geese and sandhill cranes flying high overhead. Women counted the full jars, sacks, and crocks stored in attics and root cellars, calculating meals, hoping their labors would feed their families through the long winter months. Men did the same in their barns, eyeing bins of feed corn and barrels of the mangels (large, coarse beets) or rutabagas set aside for the cow. The families had done their best, and ready or not, winter was upon them.

"Here we had an opportunity to enjoy nature in her primitive beauty. A mild southerly breeze rustled the leaves of the trees, which had already begun to fade as if wishing to warn us that the sterner seasons of fall and winter were not far away." (Søren Bache Diary, September 22, 1844)

Autumn usually came all too soon for busy farm families. With days getting shorter, afternoons rich with slanting golden light were to be savored.

Wild game provided fresh meat, and the promise of special meals
for Thanksgiving or Christmas.

Everyone took advantage of the last warm days to get as many
outdoor tasks done as possible.

Families felt enormous relief when their grain was safely harvested, but threshing was a slow process when done with a flail.

Workers swung the flail in a circular motion so the short swingle, attached to the longer handle with a looped leather thong, struck spread grain with *just* enough force to loosen the kernels.

Experienced workers developed an easy cadence as they circled the grain.
On threshing days, rhythmic thumps echoed over the farmstead.

"We have had a very fine fall so far on. The weather has been very fine and warm in the Day time and a little frost at Nights. I have got all my crops secured and so have a great many settlers here." (Edwin Bottomly, October 31, 1845, *An English Settler in Pioneer Wisconsin*)

Farmers stored wheat or rye for their own use, bagged extra to sell, and forked straw into their barns for their animals.

Some women wove coiled baskets with clean straw. Rye straw baskets were ideal for holding bread dough as it raised. The round loaves could then be flipped onto a wooden paddle and put into a brick bake oven.

"This and the following month, on some counts, are the most joyous months of the gladsome year. We now hope in earnest to gather in the results of our summer's labors, and realize the income and profits of our investments. The golden harvest is finished and gathered into pyramids and cones around our homesteads."
(*Wisconsin and Iowa Farmer and Northwestern Cultivator,* 1854)

With the frenzy of harvest past, a man might take time for a trip to the nearest village to stock up on supplies.

But with pumpkins and other
crops waiting to be harvested,
no one lingered in town.

Lucky families enjoyed delicate produce like candied citron. After being cooked in a sugar syrup, the citron melons could be stored in the syrup or dried. "We had a variety of fruits," wrote one pioneer. "My earliest recollection is of luscious fruits and huge sugar melons that simply melted in my mouth." (Mrs. Fratt, *Racine Journal-Times,* October 4, 1933)

Children spent hours carefully digging potatoes and other root crops. Full sacks could wait on the porch, out of the weather, until someone had time to store them properly. Squash and pumpkins also stored well.

Women boiled cabbage into soups or packed the green and purple heads in sand for winter use. People from many cultural backgrounds made gallons of some form of sauerkraut by slicing the heads into fine shreds, pounding them to release their juices, adding salt, and fermenting them in huge crocks.

Farmwomen tied onions and beans in strings and hung them to dry. When harvest was good, any available space might be pressed into service.

Preserving harvest bounty was a huge challenge for settlers with no access to stores—or no money to purchase groceries. Root crops were sometimes buried in straw-lined pits. As time permitted, men dug cellars into the side of a hill or beneath their home.

A well-constructed root cellar controlled humidity and temperature to make long-term storage possible. Children lugged bushels of crops to the cellars, where they were carefully packed into barrels and bins. Women checked the produce regularly during the winter, anxious to catch any sign of rot before it could spread.

After harvest, farmers eyed the sky, sniffed for hint of storm, and hurried to prepare their fields. Many planted winter wheat or rye to ensure an early spring crop. Early seedlings developed root systems quickly and were better able to choke out weeds.

Men also cleared timber, enlarging their fields . . .

. . . and ensuring a supply of firewood for the coming months of bitter cold.

Many of the season's chores—corn huskings, apple parings, wood cuttings—were shared with neighbors. Women treasured time with friends, knowing that visits might become more difficult when winter weather settled in.

Work went quickly, and women shared news while preparing a communal harvest supper.

As days shortened, neighbors gathered for community feasts. "Mother prepared many good things," wrote one settler of harvest suppers, "among them a cool drink made from the juice of ripe currants which we raised by the bushel. Well smoked sausages were devoured in quantity. For this occasion mother usually made Swiss cookies baked in deep fat and sprinkled with sugar." (Rose Schuster Taylor, born 1863; *Wisconsin Magazine of History*, March 1945)

Social gatherings in ethnic enclaves featured favorite dishes from the Old Country. Neighbors in more diverse settlements might get their first glimpse—and taste—of a different culture while sampling unfamiliar treats.

After young people husked corn and flirted by moonlight, a family might have many bushels of corn still needing attention. Mechanical corn shellers made short work of a job that had kept families busy throughout earlier winters.

"We have two oxen to do our work, two cows to calve, one young steer and one bull, 16 ducks, and 6 hogs that we feed a little during the summer nights and during the day they go into the woods where they fare fine and if then in September we shut them up and feed them indian [*sic*] corn they are big and fat by November." (Gerard Brandt letter, March 30, 1853)

Huge cauldrons performed many functions on a farm—boiling maple sap, soaking laundry, simmering apple butter. When temperatures dropped in late autumn, men rolled the cauldrons from storage for one of the biggest jobs of the year: scalding hogs at butchering time. Scalding softened the hog's bristles, which could then be scraped off.

The whole family helped process the meat. "When hogs were killed some roasts were cut up, partly cooked and placed in stone jars," one settler explained. "Hot lard . . . was poured over them and later on, as the lard was used, the roasts were taken out as fresh and sweet as when they were first packed." (The Rambler, *Richland Center Democrat,* March 12, 1924)

Nothing was wasted. Farm-wives used intestines for sausage casings.

Once women had a new supply of clean lard, they made soap. They leached water through barrels of ashes to produce lye. The lye was cooked with lard. When thick, the mixture was poured into a wooden box to cool, resulting in a fine soap that hardened as it aged.

Butchering season also allowed families to make candles. Pioneers preferred to use tallow from sheep or cattle, which was firmer than lard. If the maker remembered to wax the inside of the mold, the candles, once cool, were easily removed. "All in all this was a cheap form of light," one man noted. "A dollar would furnish tallow for many candles. But we did not have much light. . . . One candle power at a time was our custom." (Oscar Hallam, *Minnesota History*, June 1946)

Early arrivals, perhaps still working toward the purchase of their first piglet, ate squirrel and rabbit.

People who'd lived on game for a year or more eagerly anticipated their first meal of stewed or roasted chicken.

Those with established flocks of chickens butchered any birds no longer needed or useful for egg production.

Late autumn days brought a hush to the farms. Crops, meager or bountiful, were safely gathered. Settlers knew that ready or not, winter would soon bear down.

And in autumn's last still moments, immigrants may have found time to think—
of the homes they left behind, of dreams still to fulfill.

# WINTER

"There was a world of comfort and good cheer in those
forest homes. I doubt if any child in modern palaces enjoys
happier hours than were mine on winter evenings, when
resting on the broad stone hearth in front of the big fire
place, with its blazing four-foot log, the dog on one side and
the cat on the other, my father told stories that had to be
repeated as the stock ran out, and I was gradually lulled to
sleep by the soft thunder of my mother's spinning wheel."
*(Edwin Delos Coe, "Reminiscences of a Pioneer")*

Winter arrived, soft as a new snowfall or fierce as a furious wind. White-tailed deer bucks shed their antlers. Rabbit and turkey tracks crisscrossed the farmyards, and great horned owls called at twilight. Days grew short. Temperatures plunged. For most of the Yankee and European immigrants who settled the Upper Midwest, the first winter or two could only be endured.

Some travelers, especially those who'd arrived in autumn, found only dubious shelter. Nils Gilderhus, who left Norway in 1839, shared a dugout with two other men. Relatives arrived late in 1841, and two more Norwegian men in need of lodging appeared. Six men, one woman, and two children spent that winter in the dugout.[1]

The families huddled in tiny cabins sometimes fared little better. Women hung rag rugs over empty door frames and tacked squares of greased muslin in glassless windows. Men with no access to matches struggled to keep their fires perpetually alight. Ice crystals glittered on interior walls. Wide-eyed children listened to wolves howling at night, and burrowed under quilts each morning until someone swept away snow that had sifted through the rafters overnight. "Water froze in our glasses on the table," recalled Hannah Parker, "and if a little spilled on the floor it would freeze before we could wipe it up. We had no crib for the baby and had to keep him tied in a chair. Our mother was sick all winter and we hung quilts and blankets around the stove pipe and fixed her bed in the closure."[2]

Søren Bache, welcoming new arrivals from Norway, wrote, "The joy of seeing old friends in so distant a land can surely be appreciated by anyone." Still, in crammed cabins, where a married couple might sleep with a second pair on the floor beneath the bed, nerves must have frayed; tempers must have flared. "Not all the people in the house could find a place around the stove at the same time," wrote Bache, "and the ones who got there first . . . enjoyed rights of priority. We almost perished from cold both indoors and out during the bitter winter days."[3] A Pierce County man echoed in 1856, "We have had a tremendous hard winter."[4]

In the most brutal cold, one crop still beckoned: timber. Even penniless souls could barter shingles or chopped wood for food. One Danish woman recalled, "Soon it was winter, and not having any money my husband and I had to go to work again. We helped each other to make cord wood for which we received sixty cents a cord. We had to wade through snow knee-deep and yet had to work every day the weather permitted it—it was necessary to live."[5] Some men warmed themselves by girdling trees, hacking at brush, and restocking the ever-dwindling woodpile. Others split thousands of rails while dreaming of building fences around their *own* land in the spring. Families worked together to clear the trees they'd quickly girdled and left to die months before.

Harsh weather made any labor more difficult. Women made "pacs" by sewing patch over patch onto thick woolen stockings; the layers helped in bitter weather but required daily repair. A Dutch boy and his father improvised homemade gaiters for outdoor work: "[We] tacked a piece of cloth to our wooden shoes and tied strings together around our legs below the knee to prevent the snow from falling into our shoes," he explained.[6] Some people carried boards to stand on while swinging ax or grub hoe in the snow.

But in time, the earliest cabins were replaced with larger homes of log, brick, or sawn lumber, the fear of freezing or starving to death eased, and still winter days offered time for nonessential activities. Neighbors organized sewing bees, singing schools, and educational gatherings. "Debates were usually attended by men and boys," one settler wrote, "but one evening when the question of woman's suffrage was discussed, the women attended also."[7]

Settlers isolated on farms relished trips to town. The most rural families approached the annual fall trek to town with great care, knowing whatever provisions they purchased must last for months. For settlers living closer to a village, more frequent trips for Sunday service, oyster dinners, or Christmas celebrations kept loneliness at bay.

Winter also gave children time to attend school; even the older boys were permitted to go once all corn was shucked. "We used to get pretty cold on winter mornings, wandering through the deep snow and with the temperature 20 or 30 degrees below zero," Angela Favell remembered.[8] Teachers boarding nearby, charged with lighting fires before students arrived, floundered through drifts in the bluish hush of dawn. Children who huddled near the stove during lessons built ski ramps and snow forts at recess. The schoolhouse was often pressed into service for evening classes and gatherings. Spelling bees were competitive and entertaining, and neighboring communities challenged each other to matches.

Everyone eagerly awaited the first sleigh rides. Parents bundled their children, filled their wagon bed with straw, and heated stones for foot warmers. Once everyone was settled, they flew away to visit friends, with harnesses jingling and runners *shushh*-ing on icy trails. Women vied to prepare the most savory supper. Children were astonished to discover how quickly an evening filled with stories, songs from the Old Country, and games could pass.

For teens and courting couples, the slackened workload and snowy roads made for especially fond memories. One man recalled "the crack of the driver's whip as the horses started off, the jingle of bells, the sharp, crisp winter air, the joyful songs and bandying of jokes. . . . Usually you went to some town fifteen or twenty miles away. . . . You rode all evening and probably reached the inn by 1 o'clock. Then came the oyster stew. . . . You sat around the stove, telling stories, singing songs and cracking jokes for a while. Then back home. If you were lucky and there weren't any drifts, you got home before daylight."[9]

Winter was ultimately a time to savor a slower pace, to reflect and plan, to spend quiet evenings with loved ones. "In our family it was customary to gather a lot of walnuts, butternuts, hickory and hazel nuts," an early Richland County settler wrote, "and many a winter evening we children spent in front of the fire place on the bear skin cracking nuts on the stone hearth and popping corn in a skillet over a bed of live coals."[10] The frenzy of autumn harvest was past. Women and men caught their breath, pulled rocking chairs close to the stove, and waited for spring.

SANDRA MATSON

Settlers, acutely attuned to their environment, sometimes recorded the changing seasons with eloquence in diaries and letters. "Summer with all its beauty is now gone, and today winter announces its arrival by spreading a sheet of snow over the earth," wrote Søren Bache. "With the fall of snow, a silence also seems to settle over everything. No more do we hear the song of the birds or the tinkling of cow bells. Nature has fallen asleep under her blanket of snow until spring again should stir her from her slumbers." (Søren Bache Diary, November 22, 1845)

SANDRA MATSON

During the pioneer era, immigrants who arrived in autumn desperately sought shelter where they could wait out the winter. Settlers often opened their tiny cabins to new arrivals, especially those from the Old Country. Everyone took comfort in the company of others who spoke the same language.

With endless hours to fill and few diversions, women did not take simple tools like a drop spindle—and the luxury of wool to spin—for granted.

Maintaining a fire was crucial for survival. "Only those who have experienced it can imagine the loneliness of the first winter 30 miles from a post-office," wrote one man. "One wild, windy night Mr. Gardner's fireplace went out. Soon Mr. Salisbury came. He, too, had lost fire. Together they started for Moses Smith's to borrow coal. Mr. Salisbury fell into a river when crossing on a fallen tree. While Mr. Salisbury remained at Smith's to dry his clothing, Mr. Gardner started homeward. After going some distance he thought the pail seemed light and found that the bottom had melted and the fire was gone. Returning he borrowed an iron kettle, filled it with coals, and succeeded in reaching home with it, and a good, comfortable fire greeted Mr. Salisbury on his arrival." (Helen Hicks, *Racine Journal-News*, January 15, 1932)

"The first recollection I have of anything was being awakened one bitter cold morning by my father chopping ice out of the barrel which he brought into the fireplace." (Uriah S. Hollister, *Letter and Reminiscences, 1839 and ca. 1912*)

MIKE MORBECK

Many wives and daughters did as much physical labor as their men during the first few winters. Late in life, one German-born woman told a reporter of those early years. "She shouldered an ax like all women did in those days and went into the woods with her young husband helping him fell trees and saw logs," he wrote. "She wore men's heavy boots and often the ax would glance off while she was cutting wood and cut her boots. . . . She and her sister-in-law felled trees unassisted by male help for several winters." (Nick Bruehl, *Chilton Times,* February 8, 1930) Despite the grueling labor, many women took satisfaction in their accomplishments and relished being outdoors.

Women—especially those
from Europe—helped with
barn chores as well. When
labor was done by hand,
threshing even a small crop
of grain might take all winter.

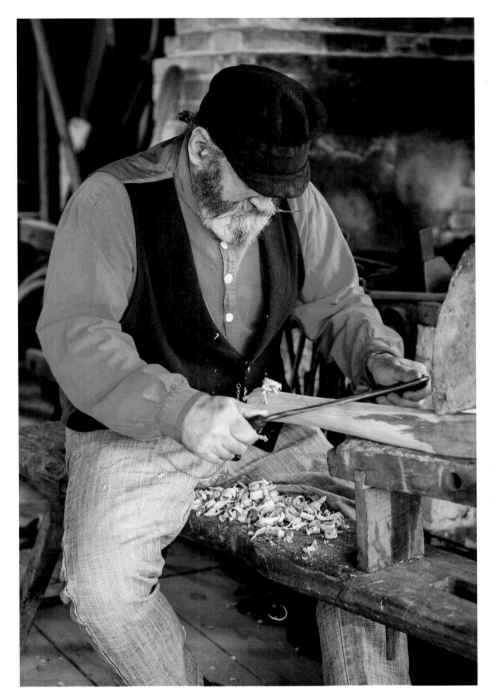

As more settlers arrived—all with homes and barns to build—men found that wood was an important cash crop. "The money [father] received from the sale of shingles kept the wolf from the door," recalled one woman (Angela Haste Favell, *Milwaukee Journal,* August 7, 1932). Hundreds or thousands of shingles could be shaped on a shaving bench during the winter months.

Once farms were established, women also had tasks to keep them busy through the coldest days. Spinning flax into linen thread allowed industrious women to spend productive hours near a stove.

Many yards of linen thread were needed to dress a big loom. Women also needed time and patience to wrap the warp threads around the loom's back beam and thread each through string eyelets called heddles—all while maintaining an even tension.

Once the loom was prepared, women wove yards of sturdy linen cloth, which was used for shirts, sheets, and towels.

Economic necessity separated some families during their first few winters—especially Finlanders and others who settled in northern Wisconsin in the late nineteenth century. When snow blanketed the farmsteads, men strapped on snowshoes and trudged off to lumber camps. With help from older children, women kept house, cared for toddlers and babies, and did all the farm chores while their husbands earned precious cash by logging.

These "wood widows" visited each other when they could, sometimes shoveling a path from one farm to the next in order to maintain that precious connection. A pot of Finnish egg coffee was kept ready for visitors.

After transitional weeks when icy mud or slush made travel difficult, settlers delighted in the first good snow. Men donned their warmest layers of clothes, harnessed their teams . . .

"January 8, 1839, a ball was given at Bark river, attended by people from Jefferson, Fort Atkinson, and Whitewater. Ball tickets were written by J. Cushman, there being no printing press except in Milwaukee. I walked ten miles to attend it, there being only enough teams to carry the ladies. I still hold my ball invitation which I prize very highly." (E. G. Fifield, *Janesville Gazette*, June 24, 1886).

MIKE MORBECK

. . . and with hot stones wrapped in quilts, set out. People commonly braved subzero temperatures for a chance to go courting or travel to town.

Trips to the nearest village provided rural settlers more than a chance to get a tool repaired or sack of wheat ground. When business slowed and village life grew quiet, innkeepers hosted eagerly anticipated dances and parties.

MIKE MORBECK

"In what better way can farmers spend the long winter evenings than by meeting together in these little classic halls to discourse topics which belong to their vocation." (*Wisconsin Farmer and Northwest Cultivator*, October 1850)

Storekeepers sold coffee and hardware, but they also shared vital news. Men often spent hours around a stove in the general store, catching up with neighbors, sharing tobacco, playing checkers.

Meetings at schools and farmers' club halls were educational and entertaining.

There was no more special time to visit friends, and attend church, than Christmas. The tiny flames of candles and oil lamps beckoned from frosty windows.

MIKE MORBECK

Children watched in wonder as Christmas Eve services unfolded in a golden glow. The wind howling around the eaves didn't seem so fierce when voices raised in song.

Christmas was also a special time to visit friends. In Yankee homes, celebrations often included a patriotic flare— especially during the Civil War.

Tabletop trees graced the parlors of well-established families, the boughs laden
with ornaments, popcorn strings, and small gifts.

Well-settled Yankee women served treats to guests on their finest china. Spalding tea cakes were iced and topped with preserved currants and a fruit cake decorated with currants and candied citron.

With secrecy and delicious anticipation, children hemmed handkerchiefs and pen wipes, stuffed pincushions, whittled toys, embroidered bookmarks with Bible verses, and planned other homemade gifts.

When Christmas and the New Year passed, families settled in for the dark, cold days of midwinter. Lamplight provided a warm glow for farmers struggling through snow-drifts from the barn.

"The planning of the barns, out-buildings, sheds and yards, so as to afford the utmost convenience, protection, and economy, requires ample study, judgment, and good taste." (*The Wisconsin Farmer,* February 1858)

After coming in from evening chores, a man might settle in to work on plans for improvements he hoped to make in the spring.

As years passed, evenings were no longer filled with chores necessary for survival. Sewing cheerful quilt tops kept women's hands busy . . . and provided the pleasure of anticipating the quilting bee that would bring neighbor women together to stitch together the quilt top, center batting, and backing.

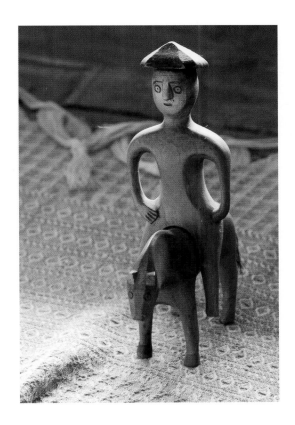

Fathers spent evenings leaning close to the woodstove, carving toys for their little ones.

"Our grandson rides in a strong gallop on a rocking horse, Schimmel, which I made for him for his last name day," wrote one man in 1855. (Dr. Louis F. Frank, comp., *The Frank-Kerler Letters, 1849–1864*; Grandfather Kerler to Grandfather Frank, Greenfield, March 1, 1855)

Few tasks were more important than writing letters to loved ones far away. If paper was scarce, people sometimes filled a page, then turned it 90 degrees and began again, crosswise. Deciphering such a letter took longer than writing it.

"Now we will go no further and must break off this our writings. . . . Live well and if we are not fortunate enough to see one another more in this world may we all meet and go forward with gladness in the next." (Gunder Asmundson Bondal, letter to Kari Evansdatter, January 17, 1854)

With stout walls and a good parlor stove, settlers enjoyed this quiet season, indulging in fancywork such as tatting lace, or reading newspapers, the Bible, or a new novel.

Each passing day provided a few more minutes of light. Women calculated time as food in their root cellars dwindled, children studied the winter term's lessons, men tended their livestock through passing storms, and everyone waited for spring.

# SECOND SPRING

"As far as I am concerned, I can, hand on heart, declare
naught else but that I thank the Lord that I am here and
regret that I did not come sooner; and when my memory
turns to many among you and I reflect how, with
your means, you could live here, I am sorry, humanly
speaking, not to have you here."
*(Johann Friederich Diederichs, January 1848)*

One morning, settlers woke to the raucous calls of red-winged blackbirds echoing from the marshes. Pasqueflowers and prairie phlox bloomed. Tree frogs and whip-poor-wills called, and coyote pups wriggled out of their dens. Immigrants stepped from cramped and smoky cabins with faces tipped toward the sun.

Settlers greeting their second spring felt a particular flush of accomplishment: they had stuck it out for a year, and now faced the next annual cycle with more experience and wisdom. This was no small feat. One German American man, while encouraging two coachmen to emigrate, put it this way: "I believe it is good for them to come here, but I also believe that they will not appreciate the first year in America. . . . I am promising them no paradise, but if they remain healthy and work hard I believe that they could stand on a different foot."[1]

One year, of course, did not a successful farm make. At best, it was achingly difficult to create a new home. But it was *possible* to create a new home, and many discovered that this place called Wisconsin truly did have much to offer. "The longer I live here the better I like the country," A. G. Tuttle wrote to his wife in Connecticut. "This is not out of the world, as many east supposed it to be. Whoever lives here ten or fifteen years will find this to be the very center of all creation."[2]

Wisconsin's promise made former European tenant farmers almost giddy. "It is almost unbelievable how fortunate it has gone for us the whole time in the new world," wrote Gunleik Asmundson Bondal. "Kari also finds herself well satisfied. Now we do not want to go back even if we were the owners of the best farm in Moland. This we know you can not believe."[3]

The seasons rolled around, and around, and around again. With uncounted strikes with grub hoe and axe blade, with untold swings of sickle or cradle scythe and flail, stubborn newcomers improved their situation. They cleared new fields and harvested crops intended for market in addition to subsistence. They built larger cabins and converted tiny shelters into granaries and summer kitchens.

Then those second cabins were replaced with brick or frame houses. Men retired handmade flails and grain cradles and invested in labor-saving reapers and mowers. Women experimented with washing machines and invested in store-bought furniture and carpets. Children lugged hand-painted immigrant trunks to their barns to be used for storing grain. Grandparents tucked their treasured Old World mementos, once packed so carefully for their long voyage, on high shelves—visible, but not handy. Those who'd immigrated as adults would sometimes look over their shoulders, missing distant family, missing their birthplace. Still, they watched their children and grandchildren grow, satisfied that the young ones would never experience the gnawing hunger and grinding poverty *they* had once known.

Gratitude, perhaps mixed with a desire to demonstrate a commitment to their new home, fixed in many foreign-born settlers the resolve to become citizens. In 1853, less than a decade after arriving, thirty-one Swiss immigrants walked to Monroe to take their oaths. Ceremony complete, the official handed each new American their citizenship paper . . . and an apple. The men and women carefully saved and planted the seeds, and the new little seedlings were known locally as "citizenship apple trees." Perhaps a gnarled old apple tree or two still grows somewhere in the hills around New Glarus, descended from those very trees nurtured by Swiss Americans so long ago.[4]

The same year, German-born Henry Frank watched dawn spread over his farm. He'd led a tumultuous life that included twelve years' service with the Foreign Legion; his mood swings sometimes worried his family. On this morning, however, all was well. He gazed over the tidy lawn and maple grove, noticed quick chicks darting away from mother hen and the spring dancing through a pasture; listened to birds singing, sheep bleating, horses whinnying. With a great sense of contentment, he began a letter to his sister. "I am looking at my nice farm from the window of the second floor," he wrote, "and everything is smiling at me."[5]

After a winter or two in the New World, immigrants understood the signs of turning seasons. Red-winged blackbirds announced their return—and spring's return—with raucous calls that echoed from marshes and sloughs.

Snow melted, and it became easier to visit friends or greet new neighbors.

Women had time to expand their gardens, and flowers bloomed among the onions and kohlrabi.

"A gravel path led from one end of our extensive garden to the other, bordered on either side with currant and gooseberry bushes, with two grapevine-covered arbors affording shade for reading, sewing, and social entertainment." (Mrs. Fratt, *Racine Journal-Times*, October 4, 1953)

Perennials, perhaps grown from bulbs or tiny slips nurtured tenderly over many miles from old home to new, grew and bloomed outside cabins. Lilacs, which perfumed the air each spring, were particular favorites. Men constructed fences, and no one spent long evenings searching for stray cattle—or lamenting garden crops lost to wild or domestic animals.

As time passed, men replaced cramped shelters with larger structures. This Norwegian cabin became a handy summer kitchen. Other tiny cabins became pigpens or granaries.

"You all told me I was foolish to leave home, but . . . we have attained the object that we left home for now by long perseverance and industry." (Letter from Margaret Douglas to her father in Scotland, November 10, 1844)

Others simply added on to their original homes, adding room as time and need dictated. Many settlers who arrived in the late nineteenth and early twentieth centuries settled in northern counties with short growing seasons, often on cutover land studded with stumps after lumber companies moved through. Those families began creating their new homes decades after the first arrivals had developed farms.

Yankee men who brought prized livestock to the Midwest proudly developed breeding programs.

"In the first place, the land (if stubble) should be plowed at a considerable depth, say ten or twelve inches. Then roll and plant the last of April or first of May, according to the weather." (*The Wisconsin Farmer,* May 1864, about corn planting)

Prosperous Yankees and established European immigrants sold their oxen and farmed with horses, which were easier to train and manage. Each new spring they turned more sod, creating new fields.

Innovations in agricultural implements continued to save farmers time and money.
In the 1860s, a garden engine like this one simplified the job of watering huge plots.

"Pursue the economical policy of employing the best labor-saving machinery. Good plows, planters, and cultivators will pay for themselves over and over again—if not left in the field to rot." (*The Wisconsin Farmer,* May 1858)

Decades later, an entrepreneur who invested in a steam engine would travel from farm to farm at threshing time.

For men who'd once spent many backbreaking hours flailing wheat and rye, steam-powered threshing rigs gobbled cut grain with jaw-dropping speed.

Women enjoyed new technology as well—sewing machines and washing machines and cream separators. The Sears, Roebuck catalog made innovations accessible even to those far from urban centers.

More often than not, the people who'd traveled so far to settle in Wisconsin came to realize that the monumental gamble of immigration had paid off. An Irish widow who survived by taking in laundry would have savored having time to knit something fancy, in her own tidy home . . .

"I think we shall be contented here." (Ellen Spaulding Miller, *Papers, 1863, 1870–1887*)

. . . and the pleasure of store-bought furniture, and china dishes for serving friends.

"Although in the spring of 1849 there was no other settler within a radius of four miles of our Fountain Lake farm, in three or four years almost every quarter-section of government land was taken up, mostly by enthusiastic home-seekers from Great Britain, with only here and there Yankee families from adjacent states, who had come drifting indefinitely westward in covered wagons, seeking their fortunes like winged seeds; all alike striking root and gripping the glacial drift soil as naturally as oak and hickory trees; happy and hopeful, establishing homes and making wider and wider fields in the hospitable wilderness." (John Muir, *The Story of My Boyhood and Youth*)

Farmers tallied success in the growth of their livestock herds, in sturdy homes and healthy, well-fed children. With hard work and a little luck, a young man with no hope of owning land in Europe might one day curry his own horse on his own farm.

Families watched their farms mature with quiet pride and satisfaction. "As a clearing matures," wrote Karl Pflaume, "it more and more resembles the cultivated fields and meadows of Europe. The originally wild appearance grows friendlier and the features grow more regular. Fruit trees grow, and when the first fence wears out it is replaced with a neater and better one." (*Wisconsin Magazine of History*, Winter 1978–1979)

All of the newcomers who flooded Wisconsin in the nineteenth century created a new place, a place not wholly severed from old homes in Denmark or Wales or Massachusetts. A portrait of President Abraham Lincoln had a place of honor on one wall in this Norwegian American home . . .

. . . while a tapestry woven
in the Old Country graced
another.

Parents and grandparents told stories to help children born in Wisconsin understand the significance of rosemaled trunks and other mementos from the Old Country. As years passed, future generations often revived Old World folk art traditions.

In a German American home, framed pieces represented the Old World, while an in-progress patchwork quilt represented the new.

Ethnicity lingered in food traditions,
such as Finnish pulla bread . . .

. . . and the puffy Danish pancakes
called aebleskivers.

Immigrants' descendants
also preserved their cultural
heritage in musical traditions
and in clothing worn on
special occasions to honor
their ancestors' homeland.

It was not easy to leave one home and create another. Those who immigrated as adults sometimes paused in reflection, thinking of the Old Country.

But longing often faded as elders watched their children and grandchildren
stretch, adapt . . . and thrive.

# PHOTOGRAPHER'S NOTE

On my first visit to Old World Wisconsin, in October 1998, I was so impressed that I turned to my wife and said, "I'm coming back." Even though I live in Seattle, I did come back; in fact, since then I have made several trips every year since to photograph the beauty of Old World and its many interesting and constantly changing activities. I wish to thank the staff for its warm hospitality on all of those visits.

Photography isn't just allowed at Old World Wisconsin, it's encouraged. Visitors are encouraged to bring their cameras and photograph anything and everything on site: the working farms, the many animals, the friendly interpreters dressed in period clothing, the nineteenth-century political debates, the reenactment of Civil War activities, and more. In fact, the Old World Wisconsin Foundation sponsors an annual photo contest with significant cash prizes for photos taken at Old World. Check the website *www.friendsoww.org* for more information, then come often and bring your camera. Old World Wisconsin is a photographer's paradise.

# NOTES

## INTRODUCTION

1. Rose Schuster Taylor, "Peter Schuster: Dane County Farmer," *Wisconsin Magazine of History* 28, no. 3 (March 1945): 280.

2. Wisconsin Historical Society, "19th-century Immigration," Turning Points in Wisconsin History, www.wisconsinhistory.org/turningpoints/tp-018/?action=more_essay.

3. The Wisconsin Cartographers' Guild, *Wisconsin's Past and Present: A Historical Atlas* (Madison: University of Wisconsin Press, 1998), 82.

4. A. G. Tuttle, "Letter Written from Fort Winnebago in 1847 by the Late A. G. Tuttle to His Wife, Then a Resident of New England, Feb. 15, 1847," *Baraboo Republic,* May 25, 1922.

5. A. G. Tuttle, "Letter Written at Madison by the Late A. G. Tuttle of Baraboo—Thinks an Injustice Was Done the Indians of State," *Baraboo Republic,* n.d. (probably 1922).

6. National Park Service, "State by State Numbers," Homestead National Monument of America, www.nps.gov/home/historyculture/statenumbers.htm.

7. Isaac T. Smith, "Early Settlement of Rock County: Journal of Isaac T. Smith, 1836," *Wisconsin Historical Collections* 6 (1872): 416.

8. Uriah S. Hollister, *Letter and Reminiscences, 1839 and ca. 1912,* June 1839, University of Wisconsin Digital Collections/State of Wisconsin Collection, http://digicoll.library .wisc.edu/cgi-bin/WI/WI-idx?id=WI.HollUri1a.

9. Søren Bache, *A Chronicle of Old Muskego: The Diary of Søren Bache, 1839–1847*, ed. and trans. Clarence A. Clausen and Andreas Elviken (Northfield, MN: Norwegian-American Historical Association, 1951), 15.

10. Mathais Duerst, "Diary of One of the Original Colonists of New Glarus, 1845," trans. John Luchsinger, *Wisconsin Historical Collections* 15 (1900): 333.

11. John and Margred Owen, "Documents: Immigrant Letters," *Wisconsin Magazine of History* 13, no. 4 (June 1930): 410.

12. Johann Schroeder, "Where Oxen Have the Speed of Horses," *Milwaukee Journal,* May 7, 1933.

13. Dr. Louis F. Frank, comp., *German-American Pioneers in Wisconsin and Michigan: The Frank-Kerler Letters, 1849–1864* (Milwaukee: Milwaukee County Historical Society, 1971), 70.

14. Ibid., 365.

15. Karl Pflaume, "A German Farmer Views Wisconsin, 1851–1863," ed. Hartmut Keil, trans. Marylou Pelzer, *Wisconsin Magazine of History* 62, no. 2 (Winter 1978–1979): 140.

16. Ole Knudsen Nattestad, "Description of a Journey to North America," ed. Rasmus Björn Anderson, *Wisconsin Magazine of History* 1, no. 2 (December 1917): 186.

17. N. G. Abbott, "Pioneer Occupations," *Baraboo News*, April 4, 1918.

18. Oscar Hallam, "A Midwest Farm Boy of the 1870s," *Minnesota History* 27, no. 2 (June 1946): 86.

19. Emeline M. Moulton, *Letters, 1846–1853,* June 14, 1846, University of Wisconsin Digital Collections/State of Wisconsin Collection, http://digicoll.library.wisc.edu/cgi-bin/WI/WI-idx?id=WI.Moulton1g.

20. Orpha Ranney, *Papers,* November 21, 1847, University of Wisconsin Digital Collections/State of Wisconsin Collection, http://digicoll.library.wisc.edu/cgi-bin/WI/WI-idx?id=WI.Ranney1b.

21. Zachary Cooper, *Black Settlers in Rural Wisconsin* (Madison: State Historical Society of Wisconsin, 1994), 24.

22. Caroline Howard Alter, quoted in "Reminiscences of La Crosse Given by One of Earliest Residents," comp. Lillian H. Van Auken, *La Crosse Tribune*, June 18, 1922.

23. Theodore Rodolf, "Pioneering in the Wisconsin Lead Region," *Wisconsin Historical Collections* 15 (1900): 358.

24. George M. Stephenson, ed. and trans., "Letters Relating to Gustaf Unonius and the Early Swedish Settlers in Wisconsin," *Augustana Historical Society Publications* 7 (1937): 43.

25. Mabel V. Hansen, "The Swedish Settlement on Pine Lake," *Wisconsin Magazine of History* 7, no. 1 (September 1924): 48.

26. Hallam, "A Midwest Farm Boy of the 1870s," 86–87.

27. Frank, *German-American Pioneers in Wisconsin and Michigan*, 187.

## SPRING

1. Lillian Krueger, "Motherhood on the Wisconsin Frontier," *Wisconsin Magazine of History* 29, no. 2 (December 1945): 157.

2. Rose Schuster Taylor, "Peter Schuster: Dane County Farmer," *Wisconsin Magazine of History* 28, no. 3 (March 1945): 289.

3. Uriah S. Hollister, *Letter and Reminiscences, 1839 and ca. 1912,* June 1839, University of Wisconsin Digital Collections/State of Wisconsin Collection, http://digicoll.library.wisc.edu/cgi-bin/WI/WI-idx?id=WI.HollUri1a.

4. Ellen Spaulding Miller, *Papers, 1863, 1870–1887,* May 16, 1870, University of Wisconsin Digital Collections/State of Wisconsin Collection, http://digital.library.wisc.edu/1711.dl/wiarchives.uw-whs-ec00bf.

5. Bernard J. Cigrand, "Parental Stories of Pioneer Times," newspaper unknown, April 29, 1916.

6. Evelyn McClintock, "History of the Downer Family," *La Crosse Tribune*, June 20, 1926.

7. Cigrand, "Parental Stories of Pioneer Times."

## SUMMER

1. Søren Bache, *A Chronicle of Old Muskego: The Diary of Søren Bache, 1839–1847* (North-field, MN: Norwegian-American Historical Association, 1951), 38. A *skippund* equals about 350 pounds.
2. George M. Stephenson, ed. and trans., "Letters Relating to Gustaf Unonius and the Early Swedish Settlers in Wisconsin," *Augustana Historical Society Publications* 7 (1937): 47.
3. *Wisconsin Farmer and Northwest Cultivator* 8, no. 8 (August 1856).
4. Frederick O. Honajager, "Experiences of a Waukesha County Pioneer Farmer Boy," *Waukesha Freeman*, May 11, 1921.
5. Celina Peckham Wood, "Recalls Pioneer Days," newspaper unknown, February 1927.
6. Honajager, "Experiences of a Waukesha County Pioneer Farmer Boy."
7. W. F. Winsey, "Maple Creek Pioneer Remembers When Bears Raided Farmers' Yards," *Appleton Post-Crescent*, October 26, 1923.
8. Johann Schroeder, "Where Oxen Have the Speed of Horses," *Milwaukee Journal*, May 7, 1933.
9. Uriah S. Hollister, *Letter and Reminiscences, 1839 and ca. 1912,* June 1839, University of Wisconsin Digital Collections/State of Wisconsin Collection, http://digicoll.library .wisc.edu/cgi-bin/WI/WI-idx?id=WI.HollUri1a.
10. Dr. Louis F. Frank, comp., *German-American Pioneers in Wisconsin and Michigan: The Frank-Kerler Letters, 1849–1864* (Milwaukee: Milwaukee County Historical Society, 1971), 185.
11. Ibid.

## AUTUMN

1. W. F. Winsey, "Freedom Pioneer Lived on Same Farm All His Lifetime," *Appleton Crescent*, October 13, 1923.
2. George W. Morrison, "Tell Tales of Pioneer Days," *Portage Democrat*, June 8, 1905.
3. Ingeborg Holdahl Alvstad, *Reminiscences—Pioneer Days in Wisconsin,* University of Wisconsin Digital Collections/State of Wisconsin Historical Collection, http://digital .library.wisc.edu/1711.dl/WI.Alvstad2d, 3.
4. Johann Schroeder, "Where Oxen Have the Speed of Horses," *Milwaukee Journal,* May 7, 1933.
5. Ellen Spaulding Miller, *Papers, 1863, 1870–1887,* December 20, 1874, University of Wisconsin Digital Collections/State of Wisconsin Collection, http://digital.library.wisc.edu /1711.dl/wiarchives.uw-whs-ec00bf, 101–102.
6. The Rambler, "Intimate Incidents of Pioneer Life in Richland County," *Richland Center Democrat*, March 12, 1924.
7. Frances Clements, "A Bohemian Family on St. Joseph's Ridge," *La Crosse Tribune*, June 6, 1926.

8. Rose Schuster Taylor, "Peter Schuster: Dane County Farmer," *Wisconsin Magazine of History* 28, no. 3 (March 1945): 288.

9. Mrs. Edward Collins, "Memories of a Pioneer Woman," newspaper unknown, 1898.

10. Winsey, "Freedom Pioneer Lived on Same Farm All His Lifetime."

## WINTER

1. Mrs. Styrk Reque, "Mrs. Styrk Reque Tells History of Early Pioneers of Gilderhus Clan," *Capital Times* (Madison), September 7, 1930.

2. Mrs. Hannah L. Parker, "Pioneer Life in Waushara County," *Wautoma Argus*, March 5, 1924.

3. Søren Bache, *A Chronicle of Old Muskego: The Diary of Søren Bache, 1839–1847* (Northfield, MN: Norwegian-American Historical Association, 1951).

4. William Hodges, *Letter,* June 11, 1856, University of Wisconsin Digital Collections/State of Wisconsin Collection, http://digital.library.wisc.edu/1711.dl/WI.Hodges1i.

5. Thomas P. Christensen, "Danish Settlement in Wisconsin," *Wisconsin Magazine of History* 12, no. 1 (September 1928): 27.

6. Fr. Verwyst, "Struggles of Religious Pioneer in Norway Wis. Told by Fr. Verwyst," *Superior Telegram*, October 20, 1916.

7. Franklin E. Swett, quoted in "Recall Pioneer Days in County," *Fond du Lac Commonwealth,* March 25, 1909.

8. Angela Haste Favell, "A Girl Pioneer in the Wisconsin Wilderness: Grandmother's Story of her Childhood in the 'Big Woods' 75 Years Ago," *Milwaukee Journal*, August 7, 1932.

9. "Pioneer Milwaukeeans Recall Their Old Courtin' Days," *Milwaukee Journal*, December 26, 1920.

10. The Rambler, "Intimate Incidents of Pioneer Life in Richland County," *Richland Center Democrat*, March 19, 1924.

## SECOND SPRING

1. Dr. Louis F. Frank, comp., *German-American Pioneers in Wisconsin and Michigan: The Frank-Kerler Letters, 1849–1864* (Milwaukee: Milwaukee County Historical Society, 1971), p. 247.

2. Tuttle, A. G., "How a Pioneer Saw This Country, 1847, a Poisoned Wolf," *Baraboo Republic,* January 15, 1921.

3. Gunleik Asmundson Bondal, *Letter,* 1854, University of Wisconsin Digital Collections/ State of Wisconsin Collection, http://digital.library.wisc.edu/1711.dl/WI.Bondal2m.

4. Elda and Linda Schiesser, *The Swiss Endure: 1845–1995* (New Glarus, WI: E. Schiesser, 1994).

5. Frank, *German-American Pioneers in Wisconsin and Michigan*, 216.

# BIBLIOGRAPHY

Abbott, N. G. "Pioneer Occupations." *Baraboo News*, April 4, 1918. (Wisconsin Local History and Biography Articles at wisconsinhistory.org; henceforth cited as WLHBA)

Aldrich, Hannah. "Hannah's Letters: The Story of a Wisconsin Pioneer Family, 1856–1864." *Wisconsin Magazine of History* 74, no. 3 (Spring 1991): 162–195.

Alter, Caroline Howard, in "Reminiscences of La Crosse Given by One of Earliest Residents," comp. Lillian H. Van Auken. *La Crosse Tribune*, June 18, 1922.

Alvstad, Ingeborg Holdahl. *Reminiscences—Pioneer Days in Wisconsin & Earliest Experiences.* University of Wisconsin Digital Collections/State of Wisconsin Collections, http://digital.library.wisc.edu.

Bache, Søren. *A Chronicle of Old Muskego: The Diary of Søren Bache, 1839–1847.* Northfield, MN: Norwegian-American Historical Association, 1951.

Bondal, Gunleik Asmundson. *Letter, 1854.* University of Wisconsin Digital Collections/State of Wisconsin Collections, http://digicoll.library.wisc.edu.

Bottomly, Edwin. "An English Settler in Pioneer Wisconsin." *Wisconsin Historical Collections* 25 (1918).

Brandt, Gerard. *Letter, 1853.* University of Wisconsin Digital Collections/State of Wisconsin Collections.

Bremer, Fredrika, in *Swedes in Wisconsin* by Frederick Hale. Madison: State Historical Society of Wisconsin, 2002.

Bruehl, Nick. "A Pioneer Settler" (re Margaretha Schwalback). *Chilton Times*, February 8, 1930. (WLHBA)

"Came to Cicero When Oxen Trod Forest Trail." *Appleton Post-Crescent*, February 9, 1924. (WLHBA)

Christensen, Thomas P. "Danish Settlement in Wisconsin." *Wisconsin Magazine of History* 12, no. 1 (September 1928): 19–40.

Cigrand, Bernard J. "Parental Stories of Pioneer Times" (re Waubeka). Newspaper unknown, April 29, 1916. (WLHBA)

Clark, Mrs. Mary M. "Ways of Living in Sixties Are Described by Pioneer: Elaborate Stores of Home Prepared Food Were Accumulated for Winter." *Antigo Daily Journal*, January 25, 1930. (WLHBA)

Clements, Frances. "A Bohemian Family on St. Joseph's Ridge." *La Crosse Tribune,* June 6, 1926.

Coe, Edwin Delos. "Reminiscences of a Pioneer in the Rock River Country." *Proceedings of the State Historical Society of Wisconsin* 55 (1908): 189–203.

Collins, Pat. "Buck and Bright, Faithful Oxen, Helped Pioneer Carve Out Farms." *Antigo Daily Journal,* April 2, 1930. (WLHBA)

Collins, Mrs. Edward. "Memories of a Pioneer Woman." Newspaper unknown, 1898. (WLHBA)

Cooper, Zachary. *Black Settlers in Rural Wisconsin.* 2nd ed. Madison: State Historical Society of Wisconsin, 1994.

Diederichs, Johann Friederich. In *Germans in Wisconsin,* by Richard H. Zeitlin. Madison: State Historical Society of Wisconsin, 2000.

Dorschner, Chester. "Pioneer Recalls Early Days in Dale and Medina." *Appleton Post-Crescent,* December 29, 1933. (WLHBA)

Douglas, James. *James and Margaret Douglas letters, 1840–1843, Milwaukee.* University of Wisconsin Digital Collections/State of Wisconsin Collections, http://digital.library .wisc.edu.

Downey, C. F. "Pioneer Settler Recalls Beginning of Stoughton." *Courier-Hub,* Stoughton, July 9, 1935. (WLHBA)

Duerst, Mathais. "Diary of One of the Original Colonists of New Glarus, 1845." Translated by John Luchsinger. *Wisconsin Historical Collections* 15 (1900): 292–337.

Eldred, Daniel F. "Pioneer Days Are Recalled." *Watertown Times,* April 29, 1910.

Favell, Angela Haste. "A Girl Pioneer in the Wisconsin Wilderness: Grandmother's Story of her Childhood in the 'Big Woods' 75 Years Ago." *Milwaukee Journal,* August 7, 1932.

Ferguson, Mrs. L. N. "Vivid Story of Pioneer Days." *Marinette Eagle-Star,* April 4, 1916. (WLHBA)

Fifield, E. G. "Early Pioneers: The Early Settlers of the Rock River Valley." *Janesville Gazette,* June 24, 1886. (WLHBA)

Fowler, D. W. "Pioneer Life Stories." *Milwaukee Sunday Sentinel,* February 8, 1891. (WLHBA)

"Fox Lake Pioneer Made Trip from Ireland to America as Mere Child." (re Mary Adelaide Carroll). *Beaver Dam Daily Citizen,* December 23, 1932. (WLHBA)

Frank, Dr. Louis F., compiler. *German-American Pioneers in Wisconsin and Michigan: The Frank-Kerler Letters, 1849–1864.* Milwaukee, WI: Milwaukee County Historical Society, 1971.

Fratt, Mrs. "Paper on Pioneer Days by Mrs. Fratt." *Racine Journal-Times,* October 4, 1933. (WLHBA)

Garland, Hamlin. *A Son of the Middle Border.* New York: Penguin Books, 1995.

Gerard, Norman. "Pioneer Days: An Interesting Paper from the Pen of Mr. Norman Gerard of Stoughton, Wis, who was an Early Omro Settler." *Omro Herald,* June 25, 1910. (WLHBA)

Goodell, N. S. "Pioneer of the Many Pioneers." *Sheboygan Press,* January 16, 1915. (WLHBA)

Hallam, Oscar. "A Midwest Farm Boy of the 1870s." *Minnesota History* 27, no. 2 (June 1946): 83–95.

Hansen, Mabel V. "The Swedish Settlement on Pine Lake." *Wisconsin Magazine of History* 8, no. 1 (September 1924): 38–51.

Hastings, Lucy A. *Family Correspondence, 1838, 1855–1874*. University of Wisconsin Digital Collections/State of Wisconsin Collections, http://digicoll.library.wisc.edu.

Herzog, Henry. "Respected Pioneer Tells of Early Days in Sheboygan County." *Sheboygan Press*, January 18, 1918. (WLHBA)

Hicks, Helen. "Pioneer Settler of Spring Prairie was New York Man." *Racine Journal-News*, January 15, 1932. (WLHBA)

"History of Scotch Pioneers in Waukesha County Dates Back to Wilderness Days." *Waukesha Daily Freeman*, September 16, 1943. (WLHBA)

Holand, Hjalmar R. "A Remarkable Pioneer." *Door County Democrat* (Sturgeon Bay), June 23, 1916.

Hodges, William. *Letter, June 11, 1856*. University of Wisconsin Digital Collections/State of Wisconsin Collection, http://digicoll.library.wisc.edu.

Hollister, Uriah S. *Letter and reminiscences, 1839 and ca. 1912*. University of Wisconsin Digital Collections/State of Wisconsin Collections, http://digicoll.library.wisc.edu.

Honajager, Frederick O. "Experiences of a Waukesha County Pioneer Farmer Boy." *Waukesha Freeman*, May 11, 1921. (WLHBA)

Huey, Mrs. Thomas. *Address, 1924* (transcriptions). University of Wisconsin Digital Collections/State of Wisconsin Collections, http://digital.library.wisc.edu.

Illichman, S. J. "Pioneer Czech Settlers of Langlade County." *Antigo Daily Journal*, March 25, 1933. (WLHBA)

"Interesting Life of Aged Pioneer" (re Anton Emmerich, shoemaker). *Merrill Daily Herald*, September 14, 1921. (WLHBA)

Kittleson, Thor. "Old Pioneer Sketches the Frontier Days." *Blanchardville Blade*, August 2, 1926. (WLHBA)

Kohl, John C. "Pioneer Tells of Early Life in Marshfield and Its Surroundings." *Marshfield News-Herald*, January 19, 1931. (WLHBA)

Krueger, Lillian. "Motherhood on the Wisconsin Frontier." *Wisconsin Magazine of History* 29, no. 2 (December 1945): 157–183.

Krynski, Elizabeth, and Kimberly Little, ed. "Hannah's Letters: The Story of a Wisconsin Pioneer Family, 1856–1864." *Wisconsin Magazine of History* (Spring 1991): 39–62.

"La Crosse Long Ago: A Series of Stories of the Pioneers Entered in the Prize Contest of the La Crosse County." *La Crosse Tribune*, May–July 1926. (WLHBA)

Little, J. M. "Pioneer Days." *Ripon Free Press*, December 16, 1886. (WLHBA)

Mather, Channing. "Days of Pioneer Mothers in Sheboygan County Are Described by Mr. (Channing) Mather." *Sheboygan Press*, May 11, 1929. (WLHBA)

McClintock, Evelyn. "History of the Downer Family." *La Crosse Tribune*, June 20, 1926.

Miller, Ellen Spaulding. *Papers, 1863, 1870–1887* (transcriptions). University of Wisconsin Digital Collections/State of Wisconsin Collections, http://digicoll.library.wisc.edu.

Morrison, George W. "Tell Tales of Pioneer Days." *Portage Democrat,* June 8, 1905. (WLHBA)

Moulton, Emeline M. *Letters, 1846–1853.* University of Wisconsin Digital Collections/State of Wisconsin Collections, http://digicoll.library.wisc.edu.

"Mrs. Styrk Reque Tells History of Early Pioneers of Gilderhus Clan." *Capital Times* (Madison), September 7, 1930. (WLHBA)

Muir, John. *The Story of My Boyhood and Youth.* New York: Atlantic Monthly Company, 1912.

Nattestad, Ole Knudsen. "Description of a Journey to North America," ed. Rasmus Björn Anderson. *Wisconsin Magazine of History* 1, no. 2 (December 1917): 149–186.

Ostrander, J. W. "A Letter from One of Our Earliest Pioneers." *Waterloo Democrat,* September 8, 1905. (WLHBA)

Owen, John and Margred. "Documents: Immigrant Letters." *Wisconsin Magazine of History* 13, no. 4 ( June 1930): 409–416.

"Ox Team and Pioneer Ways Described by Racine Woman, Aged 88" (re Hannah Caystile). *Racine Call,* February 28, 1923. (WLHBA)

Parker, Mrs. Hannah L. "Pioneer Life in Waushara County." *Wautoma Argus,* February 13, February 20, March 5, March 12, 1924. (WLHBA)

Parson, Ruben L. *Ever the Land: A Homestead Chronicle.* Staples, MN: Adventure Publications, 1978.

Pflaume, Karl. "A German Farmer Views Wisconsin, 1851–1863," ed. Hartmut Keil, trans. Marylou Pelzer. *Wisconsin Magazine of History* 62, no. 2 (Winter 1978–1979), 128–143.

"Pioneering in Early Days" (re Joseph Anderson). *Washburn Times,* February 22, 1923. (WLHBA)

"Pioneer Life in Fond Du Lac." No year. Newspaper unknown. (WLHBA)

"Pioneer Milwaukeeans Recall Their Old Courtin' Days." *Milwaukee Journal,* December 26, 1920. (WLHBA)

Rambler, The. "Intimate Incidents of Pioneer Life in Richland County." *Richland Center Democrat,* March 12, March 19, April 2, and April 9, 1924. (WLHBA)

"Recall Pioneer Days in County." *Fond du Lac Commonwealth,* March 25, 1909. (WLHBA)

Rodolf, Theodore. "Pioneering in the Wisconsin Lead Region." *Wisconsin Historical Collections* 15 (1900).

Schiesser, Elda, and Linda Schiesser. *The Swiss Endure: 1845–1995.* New Glarus, WI: E. Schiesser, 1994.

Sherpe, Howard. "A Rough Beginning: The Struggles of Norwegian Immigrant Families." *Vesterheim* 11, no. 1 (2013).

Schroeder, Johann. "Where Oxen Have the Speed of Horses." *Milwaukee Journal,* May 7, 1933. (WLHBA)

Simmons, H. M. "Pioneer Life in Kenosha County." Newspaper unknown, October 5, 1881. (WLHBA)

Smith, Isaac T. "Early Settlement of Rock County: Journal of Isaac T. Smith, 1836." Wisconsin Historical Collections 6 (1872).

"Smith's Coulee Pioneers Began Night School Study More Than Half Century Ago Records Show." *La Crosse Tribune* & *Leader-Press*, March 22, 1931.

Stephenson, George M., trans. and ed. "Letters Relating to Gustaf Unonius and the Early Swedish Settlers in Wisconsin." *Augustana Historical Society Publications* 7, 1937.

"Stories of Pioneers." *Fond du Lac Bulletin*, December 15, 1907. (WLHBA)

Stortroen, Anders Jensen, in *Norwegians in Wisconsin* by Richard J. Fapso. Madison: State Historical Society of Wisconsin, 2001.

Taylor, Rose Schuster. "Peter Schuster, Dane County Farmer." *Wisconsin Magazine of History* 28, no. 3 (March 1945):

Tuttle, A. G. "How a Pioneer Saw This Country, 1847, a Poisoned Wolf." *Baraboo Republic*, January 15, 1921. (WLHBA)

———. "Letter Written from Fort Winnebago in 1847 by the Late A. G. Tuttle to His Wife, Then a Resident of New England." *Baraboo Republic*, May 25, 1922. (WLHBA)

———. "Letter Written at Madison by the Late A. G. Tuttle of Baraboo—Thinks an Injustice Was Done the Indians of State." *Baraboo Repulbic*, n.d. (WLHBA)

Verwyst, Fr. "Struggles of Religious Pioneer in Norway Wis. Told by Fr. Verwyst." *Superior Telegram*, October 20, 1916. (WLHBA)

Whitchurch, Anna Kellman. "My Grandparents Came from Sweden." *Wisconsin Magazine of History* 35, no. 3 (Spring 1952): 170–176.

Whyte, Dr. "Pioneer Tells of Early Struggles with Wilderness." *Milwaukee Sentinel*, November 12, 1922. (WLHBA)

Winsey, W. F. "Freedom Pioneer Lived on Same Farm All His Lifetime" (re Cornelius De Jong). *Appleton Crescent*, October 13, 1923. (WLHBA)

———. "Maple Creek Pioneer Remembers When Bears Raided Farmers' Yards" (re Mrs. Herman Nass). *Appleton Post-Crescent*, October 26, 1923. (WLHBA)

Winterbotham, Mrs. Ann. "Mrs. Ann Winterbotham's Life Typical of the Wisconsin Pioneers." *Madison Democrat*, February 14, 1915. (WLHBA)

*Wisconsin and Iowa Northwestern Cultivator* IV, no. 9 (Sept. 1854): 210.

Wood, Celina Peckham. "Recalls Pioneer Days" (re Grant County). Newspaper unknown, February 1927. (WLHBA)

# INDEX

Note: page numbers in **bold** indicate photos